Adventure Curriculum for Physical Education

MIDDLE SCHOOL

BY

Jane Panicucci

WITH

Lisa Faulkingham Hunt
Amy Kohut
Alison Rheingold
Nancy Stratton

Acknowledgments

I would like to acknowledge and honor the high-performing team of Nancy Stratton, Amy Kohut, Alison Rheingold and Lisa Hunt, who were integral to the production of this curriculum. Although I have coached and trained a number of superb teams in the past, I have not been lucky enough to participate on many. This was a personal and professional luxury. The effort required to write this curriculum was powerful, productive and, most of the time, enjoyable. This team of great minds and can-do spirits provided the core content of the document, each person contributing her own unique and necessary part. The merging of these individual contributions to create the final product is where we struggled, laughed, compromised and lived our own Full Value contract. Their high performance together was nothing less than brilliant.

The core team on this project was astute enough to draw from the experiences and expertise of other professional colleagues and friends in the physical education field. A big thanks to Bill Klag Jr., Tony LaRocha and Karin Taylor for the time they spent educating us on the idiosyncrasies of middle-school children and guiding us to create a document that is user-friendly for teachers. Bill and Karin read every line of our near-final draft and provided invaluable feedback on the document itself. Special thanks also to Peggy Tuttle for helping us organize the broad scope of this work.

The internal expertise here at Project Adventure is a bottomless well of support. Thanks to Dr. Katie Kilty and Nancy Terry for reviewing this curriculum and offering honest and detailed feedback. Thanks also to Rufus Collinson, our on-staff editor, for gently supporting our project and seamlessly connecting us to Lisa French, our amazing editor, who can see more detail than my mind will ever be able to absorb. Thanks to Dick Prouty, CEO, for driving Project Adventure's core strategy of reaching out to our physical education clientele with material that will enhance their programming.

Finally, the core Physical Education Team here at Project Adventure would like to thank our clients—each educator who is implementing an Adventure program. Our knowledge of your work, and the amazing impact that it has on those whom you service, provided us with the momentum and the focus to produce this curriculum in the midst of our busy consulting schedules. Throughout the years we have learned a great deal from what you do, and it is reflected in these pages.

—Jane Panicucci
May, 2002

Contents

GRADE 6   14

Section 1: Creating Community

Section 2: Establishing Full Value Norms

Section 4: Building Trust

Section 5: Experiences Using Low Elements

Introduction

WHAT IS ADVENTURE PROGRAMMING?

Adventure is a way of doing; it is not just an activity in and of itself. If the word adventure conjures up images of things like rock climbing, rafting and parachuting, pause for a moment and imagine instead the way in which an activity is performed. A class becomes an adventure for students if there exists an element of surprise, if activities compel them into doing things they have never imagined possible. Adventure exists when there is engagement, and engagement comes from providing students with experiences that are unique and relevant. Adventure includes challenge—moments when students are on the brink of both success and failure, and where they both succeed and fail. Adventure is about taking risks—not necessarily physical risks, but emotional and "apparent" physical risks, where students see the natural consequences before them. For students to participate in any program like this, there needs to exist an atmosphere of safety, a space where students can speak their minds and push themselves to limits. There needs also to be an atmosphere of fun, real fun. Yet, all of this can exist in a class where no parachute is ever opened and no cliff ever scaled!

The curriculum outlined in this book offers a program of activities that provides your students with these opportunities and choices. Participants will have moments full of surprise and laughter. They will be able to do activities in such a way that they have "aha" experiences—discovering how powerful they are in this world, and how to enjoy being physically active. Games become important learning tools in an Adventure setting. Adventure programming is not reinventing the wheel of physical education; it is meant to supplement what already exists in the school curriculum. Adventure adds new activities, and a twist, to teaching and learning that you and your students will find exhilarating and powerful.

WHAT IS PROJECT ADVENTURE?

Project Adventure is an international nonprofit organization with a simple goal: "to bring the Adventure home." Our physical education roots are over 30 years deep, with the first program implementation (a tenth-grade physical education class) in 1971. PA's founders, former Outward Bound instructors, had experience in leading wilderness adventure trips. Struck by the power of Adventure, but understanding that it is more about doing and less about where and what one does, they developed a program that could be done in a gymnasium or on a playground field. The goal was to make Adventure accessible to people of all abilities and adaptable to many different time frames. From the moment when it was first implemented in that physical education class more than 30 years ago, the program has been a monumental success.

Physical education continues to be at the core of Project Adventure's work, with well over 2500 school-based physical education adoptions around the globe. We continue to develop new activities and props; offer training to give teachers the skills to use the Adventure medium safely and effectively; provide consultation to aid in the implementation of an effective curriculum; and all the other services necessary to develop, maintain and grow quality programs. PA adoptions range in scope from one teacher including a few activities in his or her curriculum to whole-school adoptions, where the Adventure approach is at the heart of all that the school does.

ABOUT THIS CURRICULUM

This curriculum pulls together Project Adventure's many years of physical education experience. It helps educators integrate and implement all or part of a K–12 Adventure component into an existing physical education program. PA promotes Adventure as a component of physical education; in no way do we suggest that it supplant your current curriculum, with its critical benefits of learning team—and lifetime—sport activities. As a supplement to a broader curriculum, Adventure is a very effective tool that will enhance the physical education experience and learning for students and teachers alike.

NOTE: This volume presents an Adventure-based physical education curriculum model for middle-school programs (Grades 6–8). The curriculum models for primary, elementary and high-school levels are offered in separate volumes that are also published by Project Adventure and can be obtained through the publisher.

We understand that good teaching is more than knowing a lot of interesting activities. What is taught needs to be well sequenced and tied to national, state and local standards. Moreover, teachers are busy, so a curriculum needs to be user-friendly and practical. As physical educators, we have a responsibility to teach both physical and psychosocial skills. A curriculum also needs to be flexible, changeable and adaptable to the wide variety of class sizes, class time frames and structures that exist in our schools. All of these factors are incorporated into the program presented in this book. (A list of key curriculum-related terms used in the text, along with definitions, is included in Appendix 1.)

Curriculum Structure and Connection to Standards

The physical education team at Project Adventure used Grant Wiggins and Joy McTighe's model as presented in *Understanding by Design* [1] as the basis for designing this curriculum. The program presented here also aligns with national and general state physical education standards. (Many standards are similar from state to state, so the standards that are common to multiple states have been addressed.)

There is general recognition that public education is becoming more standards-driven. The positive result of this trend is that curricula are being created and implemented that support key learning objectives for students. This standards-based structure helps in the design of programs that are relevant and specific to the needs

---

1. Grant Wiggins and Jay mcTighe, *Understanding by Design* (Alexandria, VA: ASCD, 1998).

of students at various grades and in various subjects. There are many high-quality Adventure physical education programs that do not yet address standards at all. However, such programs will inevitably begin to lose credibility with administrations and school boards, which could ultimately lead to the elimination or the minimization of physical education in school programs. Standards, therefore, are a key component supporting the structure of the curriculum outlined here.

DESIRED RESULTS, K–12. Following are the Desired Results for students engaging in the PA curriculum. These outcomes define the broad knowledge, skills and behaviors that serve as the foundation of the K-12 Adventure program. These Desired Results are defined more specifically by grade level in Appendix 2, including more detail about the specific skills and information students should acquire through participation in this program.

Students participating in a Project Adventure curriculum will be able to:

1. **Demonstrate an understanding of movement concepts and the use of motor skills.**

   Although Adventure can teach so much more than just motor skills, physical movement is central to what physical education is about. This curriculum integrates motor skill development in a subtle way; students experience and master critical motor skills in an environment that is fun and nonthreatening. The noncompetitive nature of the activities allows for more exploration of primary motor skills, which supports the varying ability levels in a class setting. No longer is learning about who can throw the ball the farthest, but about being engaged in a process where throwing happens naturally. The acquisition of motor skills is just part of the experience that captivates the students' attention.

2. **Demonstrate responsible personal and social behavior.**

   Learning how to engage with others appropriately is crucial to a student's future academic, social and professional success. ("How do I follow rules while still thinking critically about them? How do I learn when to trust someone else and when not to? How do my actions impact the group that I am a part of?") Students involved in this Adventure curriculum will have opportunities to explore such questions on a yearly basis. Students learn how to share and follow rules as they experience a process that allows them to explore, to question, to participate and to reflect on themselves.

3. **Demonstrate the ability to use effective interpersonal skills.**

   When major colleges and corporations are asked what they look for in a prospective student or employee, it inevitably boils down to someone who possesses the ability to work effectively with others, someone with leadership qualities, someone who can work well with others to solve conflicts and create solutions. They are looking for "team players." It is important that educators provide students with concrete tools that they can learn, practice and apply to future settings. The Adventure process does exactly this. Conflict is managed, the group process is reflected upon, leadership models are discussed.

4. **Demonstrate the ability to use the decision-making skills of appropriate goal setting, risk taking and problem solving.**

Most people seek opportunities to take risks. Unfortunately, they are not always positive risks. Allowing students to explore the decision-making process, to consider on a personal level which risks are and are not positive, is a key component of Adventure programming. Another crucial component of making good decisions is understanding how the risks taken impact individual and team goals. ("How does the risk I am about to take fit in with the goals I have set for myself or this team?") Ultimately, this process results in the ability to make better decisions and to solve problems more effectively.

5. **Understand that challenge, enjoyment, creativity, self-expression and social interaction are important, life-enhancing experiences and are found in Adventure activities.**

In order for students to understand that Adventure activities can be enjoyable and important life-enhancing experiences, the activities must be truly engaging, relevant and fun. This curriculum provides an array of activities that can be customized to meet the needs of all students. Because these activities are so different from traditional sports, often creative and self-expressive behaviors naturally emerge. Students may actually find themselves thoroughly enjoying looking silly, taking risks and laughing unabashedly with others.

6. **Demonstrate an understanding of and respect for differences.**

There is no time in our recent history when respecting the differences of others has been more critical. This tolerance does not come solely from reading a book or from hearing adults say that this is important. It comes also from experiencing the power in difference, from seeing the results of inclusion, from spending time with people of different abilities and backgrounds. This curriculum offers a number of activities that expose students to issues of difference in settings that are safe and reflective. The activities illustrate the subtleties of difference and the need to understand each of our roles in embracing difference. What powerful learning to take into one's future!

The six Desired Results described above are closely aligned with the National Physical Education Standards, as influenced and developed by the National Association for Sport and Physical Education (NASPE) Outcomes Committee and the national standards movement in educational reform, which state that:

A physically educated person:

1. Demonstrates competency in many movement forms and proficiency in a few movement forms.

2. Applies movement concepts and principles to the learning and development of motor skills.

3. Exhibits a physically active lifestyle.

4. Achieves and maintains a health-enhancing level of physical fitness.

5. Demonstrates understanding of and respect for differences among people in physical activity settings.

6. Understands that physical activity provides opportunities for enjoyment, challenge, self-expression and social interaction.

LESSON OBJECTIVES. The specific lesson objectives expected for each lesson appear at the beginning of each lesson. These have evolved directly from the Desired Results described previously. This linkage gives the teacher an immediate guide as to the goal of each lesson without having to sift back through the more global Desired Results.

Format

AGE GROUPS AND CORE THEMES. Four developmentally appropriate age groups have been identified in this PA curriculum. Each of these levels has its own particular thematic focus. The core themes are intended as guideposts for educators in framing and discussing the activities.

Primary (Kindergarten–Grade 2)
Kindness/Caring
Consideration
Respect for others
Appropriate trust
Working together

Elementary (Grades 3–5)
Communication
Cooperation
Expressing feelings
Appreciating diversity
Conflict resolution

Middle School (Grades 6–8)
Respect for differences
Problem solving
Self-esteem
Compassion

High School (Grades 9–12)
Leadership
Creativity
Risk taking

Grade-Specific Sections and Lessons

Each grade level is presented in a separate part of this book. Within the individual grade levels there are specific lessons, which are organized in four or five sections. An introductory section or sections about Creating Community and Establishing Full Value begins each of these grade levels.[2]

Because each school's physical education program has different requirements regarding time in class, frequency of meetings and so on, the lessons in this book are based not on timing but on lesson content. What may be a single class for the teacher with a double period may actually be two classes for the teacher whose classes meet for shorter periods of time. However, no single activity requires an unusually long period of time, as we realize that the double period is not enjoyed by many. Approximate activity times for a standard class of 25 are included in the lessons wherever feasible.

Class sizes also vary considerably from school to school. Each activity is designed to be successful with both large and small classes. Hints for how to adapt an activity to a particular class size are included.

How to Use Each Lesson

The components of each lesson are:

Overview: A brief statement giving a general sense of the lesson

Activities: Lists of activities that are included in the lesson

Lesson Objectives: Goals for the lesson

Materials: Props needed for the lesson

Specific Activity or Activities: Describes the specific activity (or activities) within the lesson; each activity description includes:

Setup: How to prepare the space and get the class ready

Framing: What to say to the class to set the stage for the activity

Procedure: The rules for the activity

Safety: Warnings or safety considerations

Discussion: Suggested questions or debriefing ideas

Tips and Comments: Other ideas or variations

Estimated Time: Approximate time needed to implement the activity with a standard class of 25 students

---

2. Full Value is described later in this Introduction in "Cornerstones of an Adventure Program."

IMPORTANT ASSUMPTIONS

Training

Implementing this curriculum requires proper training. Project Adventure suggests a comprehensive training plan that addresses the following key areas:

- Basic theory of Adventure and experiential education
- Experiencing of activities including warmups, ice-breakers, initiatives
- Facilitation and debriefing skills
- Technical skills as appropriate for the grade being taught
- Safety and risk-management skills appropriate for the grade being taught

Project Adventure offers a variety of workshops to meet these needs, including program consultation on specific guidelines and tools for properly implementing a program.

Safety

This curriculum does not include a safety manual. For detailed safety information, all educators should refer back to their own training. Written guidelines for low and high elements can also be found in Project Adventure's Safety Manual.[3] Some of the activities in this curriculum can be dangerous if conducted without proper training on the facilitator's part.

Props and Equipment

Each lesson details the props that are necessary for its related activities. This curriculum does assume that specialty props not typically found in the traditional physical education storage closet will be purchased. Project Adventure offers a number of prop packages that help make the acquisition of the necessary materials cost-effective. (See the PA catalog for a prop kit developed especially for this program.)

The curriculum contained in this book also assumes the construction, by qualified installers, of a low and high challenge course for certain grades. We understand that some schools will need to modify the curriculum based on what they already have installed or based on what they can have installed. Such modification is easily done. Our assumptions are:

Primary and Elementary (Grades K-5): No challenge course elements needed, lots of props required

Middle School (Grades 6-8): Low challenge course elements needed; some props required

High School (Grades 9-12): Low and high challenge course elements needed; some props required

---

3. Steve Webster, *Ropes Course Safety Manual: An Instructor's Guide to Initiatives and Low and High Elements* (Dubuque, IA: Kendall Hunt, 1989).

Warmups

Warmups are a critical aspect of Adventure programming. They serve to prepare students both physically and emotionally for the rest of the lesson as well as set the tone for the class. As physical educators, we assume that you will be able to select a proper warmup activity to meet the needs of your class. Consequently, the lessons included here do not include them. However, at the back of this book we have included an extensive list of warm-ups and resources to aid in building a solid repertoire of appropriate activities. (See Appendix 3 for more information on warmups.)

Use of Assessment

Assessment in physical education has historically been a controversial and potentially complex topic. This curriculum, unfortunately, does not solve the assessment dilemma. It does, however, offer a variety of assessment tools that can be adapted to your specific program. Once again, the generic nature of this curriculum prevents the actual scripting of assessment tools. However, it provides options that can be used or integrated into your existing structure. Assessment suggestions are found both in the lessons themselves and in the Assessment chapter near the end of the book, which also contains a glossary of key assessment terms used in this curriculum.

CORNERSTONES OF AN ADVENTURE PROGRAM

The success of an Adventure program lies in the development of a foundation that supports and promotes the attributes of Adventure: risk taking, fun, challenge and safety. At the base of this foundation are three very important Project Adventure cornerstones: the **Full Value Contract, Challenge by Choice,** and the **Experiential Learning Cycle.** These concepts underlie all of the activities in this curriculum. It is critical that they be kept in focus and in play while you teach and work with the PA curriculum.

The Full Value Contract

Every grade in this curriculum starts their Adventure unit by developing community and creating a Full Value Contract for the class. This is crucial to the success of the unit, because it creates an environment where students feel safe enough to take risks. The Full Value Contract serves as a structure for creating behavioral norms that everyone in the class agrees to follow, and that everyone in the class agrees to work on maintaining throughout the life of the class. The norm-setting process establishes an atmosphere of caring, of feeling connected and of feeling valued. This atmosphere is critical to students' being able to participate fully in Adventure activities.

There are many ways to develop a Full Value Contract. A number of different methods are included in the lessons in this book. However, feel free to create your own unique way of establishing this critical agreement in your class. We have included here a general guideline of developmentally appropriate ways in which to frame a traditional Full Value Contract for each age group. They are as follows:

Primary (Grades K-1)
Be Kind
Be Gentle
Be Safe

Elementary (Grades 3-5)
Play Hard
Play Fair
Play Safe

Middle School (Grades 6-8)
Be Here
Be Safe
Set Goals
Be Honest
Let Go and Move On

High School (Grades 9-12)
Be Present
Pay Attention
Speak Your Truth
Be Open to Outcomes
Create a Safe Environment

Remember: However you decide to establish your contract, consider it more a continuous process than a discrete activity. The process needs constant attention so that the contract becomes a living part of the class.

Challenge by Choice

Our more than thirty years of teaching Adventure have taught us many things. One of the most powerful lessons learned involves the use of **choice.** Coaxing young people into doing a difficult task or element teaches them only that they can be talked into doing something. On the other hand, helping students see that they have the right and ability to choose their level of challenge, and how to assess what is and isn't an appropriate level of challenge, teaches them how to make positive decisions for life. This is critical to a well-taught Adventure program.

As professionals, we have to understand that what is a challenge for one individual may be a panic-producing process for someone else. The art of our work is to present activities that offer choice to students, and then to allow students to make those choices. The Adventure process can support the use of choice as long as you, the teacher, respect and integrate Challenge by Choice into your work. This does *not* assume that you will allow students continually to opt out of activities because they have chosen not to play. It assumes that students will learn how to work safely in their "stretch zone" while avoiding situations that will put them more into their "panic zone."

Some find it easy to understand and explain Challenge by Choice in the following three-part way:

- Students have the right to choose how to participate.
- Students are asked to add value to the experience at all times.
- Students are asked to respect and value the decision of their class members.

There are some activities in this program that help specifically teach this key concept. Educators who keep the concept of Challenge by Choice in mind each moment of their Adventure work will meet with much more success than those who approach their work with the attitude that everyone must do everything!

Experiential Learning and the Experiential Learning Cycle

This Adventure curriculum is experiential and is based on the theory of experiential learning. Much of what you already do in physical education is experiential in nature. However, any experience in isolation can be just that—a game, or an isolated activity or event. As educators, it is our responsibility to provide students with the opportunity to gain as much from each experience as possible. The Experiential Learning Cycle (shown in the graphic below) explains the rationale for the activity structure that is used in the PA curriculum.

The Experiential Learning Cycle was developed from David Kolb's learning theory model.[4] Kolb highlights four phases of a learning cycle: concrete experience, reflective observation, abstract conceptualization and active experimentation. Each of these phases aligns with one of the four stages of the ELC. Kolb also identifies four basic learning styles: diverging, assimilating, converging and accommodating. Each style combines and uses different phases of the learning cycle. Varieties of learning styles in the class are provided for when teaching with Adventure and using the ELC.

Once an activity has been completed, a period of reflection (or Debriefing) helps students to draw relevance from the experience. Connecting the present experience to past experiences also enhances learning. In this curriculum, the Debrief comes in many forms. During this phase, the simple questions, "What happened in the activity?" "So, what can we learn from what occurred?" and, finally, "Now what can we do with this information?" or "How can we apply what we've learned to other areas of our lives?" provide the structure. This Debrief period can be active and involve action-oriented experiences, or it can be discussion-oriented. If no reflection period is provided, we limit the potential learning opportunities for our students. (See Appendix 4 for more Debriefing information.)

---

4. David A. Kolb, *Experiential Learning: Experience As the Source of Learning and Development* (Englewood Cliffs, NJ: Prentice Hall, 1984).

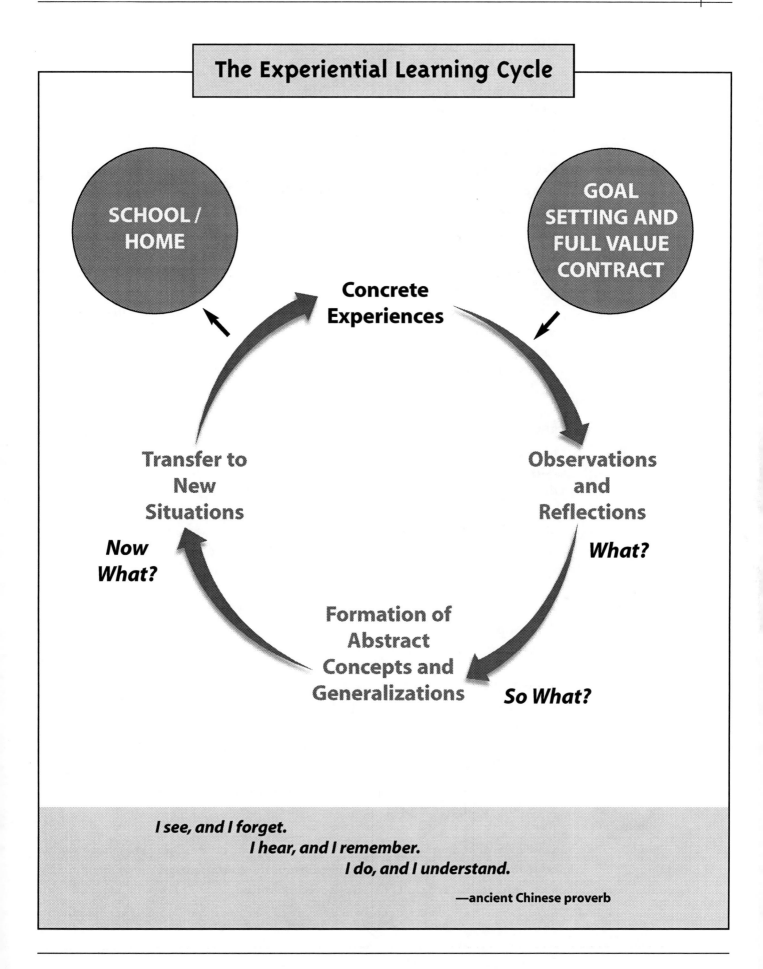

The Experiential Learning Cycle

SCHOOL / HOME

GOAL SETTING AND FULL VALUE CONTRACT

Concrete Experiences

Transfer to New Situations

Observations and Reflections

What?

Now What?

Formation of Abstract Concepts and Generalizations

So What?

I see, and I forget.
I hear, and I remember.
I do, and I understand.

—ancient Chinese proverb

GRABBing the Right Activity

This curriculum outlines a sequence of activities that we feel will be effective with a majority of standard physical education classes. However, it is impossible to predict exactly what is appropriate for every class at every stage in this program. Following is a very simple guide to help educators decide whether or not each activity in the given sequence is appropriate for their classes. The art of making a K-12 or multi-year curriculum work, however, is in "saving" some activities for later grades. If this is not respected, students participating in the same activity year after year are robbed of the spirit of wonder and surprise that so often accompanies Adventure. If you do need to GRABB another activity, try to select one of the Adventure activities that are designed to be done in your particular grade. Here are some simple questions to consider before choosing an alternative activity, or when deciding if a specific activity is appropriate. (Project Adventure uses the acronym GRABBSS to reinforce these key considerations about your students' particular situation and stage of development.)

GOALS. How does this activity relate to the goals the group has set, your goals for the lesson and your goals for the class?

READINESS. Is the group ready to do this activity? Are they emotionally and physically prepared? Do they have the necessary skills to attempt and complete the activity? If not, can the activity be altered to meet their level of readiness? Is there something that can help them increase their level of readiness?

AFFECT. What is the feeling of the group? Are they excited and energetic, or are they apathetic and low-energy? What is the level of empathy in the group? Are students at a stage where they can emotionally support each other?

BEHAVIOR. How is the group acting? Are they agreeable or disruptive? How does the group interact with each other? Are they positive or negative? Will their behavior be appropriate for this activity?

BODY. Is the group physically ready for this activity? Are they too tired, are they too hyper? If touch is involved, is that OK for this group at this time?

SETTING. What is your setting for the lesson? Are you outside? What is the weather? What are the physical conditions of the ground? Are you inside and near any obstacles? Is your space limited? Is the space quiet enough for the reflection you have chosen?

STAGE. At what stage of group development is your class in? Are they ready for a more difficult activity, or do they need to return to some basic norm setting? Do they need additional skills to work together better?

FINAL TIPS FOR TEACHERS

Leading Adventure activities can be a new experience for many physical educators. Here are some basic tips that will go a long way toward ensuring your success. In reviewing these, consider how some suggestions can also enhance your traditional physical education instruction. Remember, Adventure is not about what you do, but more about how you do it!

1. **Appear spontaneous.** Sometimes you also need to be spontaneous, but at a minimum, appear as casual as possible as you do the activities. This will keep students wondering, "What the heck will he ask us to do next?" They like the surprise element.

2. **Use this curriculum as a guide.** As mentioned already, we have put a lot of thought into the sequence of activities. However, you know your students best. Do what is appropriate using your GRABBSS guide.

3. **Be playful.** How you brief (prepare students for) an activity often sets that activity up for success or failure. If you are asking students to do something playful, join in and be playful, too. The Framing notes for each activity are just suggestions for how to brief; make your stories relevant to you and your students.

4. **Have more prepared than you think you need.** Adventure activities can be unpredictable. You never know when an activity you thought would take 30 minutes takes only 10. Have a good "bag of tricks" available so that when you have extra time, you have plenty to fill it with.

5. **Be flexible.** We can't say this enough … sometimes the right activity for the moment becomes apparent only at the last minute. Go with your gut.

6. **Don't be afraid of the discussions.** Students often like to talk! Yet, they so rarely are given chances for real reflection. Relax and go with the tenor of the conversation. If students are silent, ask better questions, or move to small-group discussions.

7. **Be communicative.** For a sequential curriculum to work, educators must keep the lines of communication open with their colleagues. Share what you are learning about what works and what doesn't so that the entire department can benefit.

8. **Keep safety in mind.** Adventure activities can go in many directions. It continues to be the teacher's responsibility to manage the safety of the class. Help students learn to manage their own safety as well.

9. **Keep the Full Value Contract, the Experiential Learning Cycle and Challenge by Choice present.** These are cornerstone principles of Adventure that are essential.

10. **Have fun!**

Adventure Curriculum for
Physical Education

Grade 6

SCOPE AND SEQUENCE

SECTION 1: CREATING COMMUNITY

Lesson 1 Working together as a new group, learning group members' names
Activities: Toss a Name
Chicken Baseball

Lesson 2 Experiencing community, exploring similarities and differences
Activities: Card Have You Ever
Monarch Tag

Lesson 3 Creating a safe environment, experimenting with cooperative versus competitive behaviors
Activities: FFEACH
Help Me Tag

Lesson 4 Working together as a group, taking care of each other's safety
Activities: Blob Tag
a.k.a. Tusker Tag

SECTION 2: ESTABLISHING FULL VALUE NORMS

Lesson 1 Learning that rules are needed for a group to function successfully
Activity: Pairs Tag

Lesson 2 Experiencing the five components of a Full Value Contract
Activities: Circle Clap
Pairs Squared
Fill the Basket
Asteroids
Transformer Tag

Lesson 3   Recognizing and identifying feelings that accompany Full Value Contract behaviors
Activity: Marketplace Relay

Lesson 4   Applying Full Value Contract concepts in the group
Activity: Warp Speed

SECTION 3: PROBLEM SOLVING

Lesson 1   Doing a problem-solving activity requiring physical skill and whole-group participation
Activity: Turnstile

Lesson 2   Reviewing the ABCDEs of Problem Solving
Activity: Don't Touch Me

Lesson 3   Performing another problem-solving activity, this time with touching
Activity: Welded Ankles

Lesson 4   Learning how to negotiate
Activity: Negotiation Squares

Lesson 5   Continuing to apply the ABCDEs of Problem Solving with resource management
and communication
Activity: Stepping Stones

SECTION 4: BUILDING TRUST

Lesson 1   Discussing trust, respecting others for making different decisions
Activities: Challenge Circles
Velcro Circle

Lesson 2   Experiencing trust and the potential lack of it, articulating ideas about what trust entails
Activities: Bumper Cars
Trust Wave

SECTION 5: EXPERIENCES USING LOW ELEMENTS

Lesson 1   Working together through physical connection, respecting differences and having
compassion for others
Activities: Balloon Trolleys
Trolleys

Lesson 2   Doing creative problem solving, supporting individual differences
Activity: TP Shuffle

Lesson 3   Problem solving, taking care of each other
Activities: Nitro Crossing

Final Lesson: Putting It All Together
Activities: Determined by facilitator

Section 1: Creating Community

LESSON 1

In this lesson, students will experience working together as a new group and will learn each other's names.

Activites
- Toss a Name
- Chicken Baseball

Lesson Objectives
Students will be able to:
- Demonstrate positive working relationships with each other
- Work together as a new group
- Recognize each person by name

Materials
- 6 throwable soft objects
- Rubber chicken

ACTIVITIES

Estimated Time

20 minutes

Toss a Name

Setup:
Ask the class to stand in a circle, shoulder to shoulder. If the class is larger than 20 students, you may want to break them into two groups. Introduce the rules first to one group, then to the other. You can float from circle to circle and guide the activity as each group completes a step.

Framing:
Say to the class, "This is an activity that will help us learn each other's names. Working well together requires that we use names rather than 'hey you' or some other attention getter. Our goal today is to learn everyone's name."

Procedure:
1. Take one tossable object, say your name, and toss it to the student on either your right or your left. That student says his or her name and tosses the object to the next person in the circle.

2. Once the object has completed the circle and everyone has said his o_
name, toss the object to a random person in the circle, but this time_
person's name first. "Here you go, Joe." This means that you have to remem_
a few names from the initial go-around. The object than moves in a random_
pattern, each "tosser" saying the name of the person to whom the object is
being tossed.

3. After everyone has tossed the object again, add a thank-you to the sequence:
"Here you go, Joe." Joe then responds, "Thank-you, Lisa." If a student can't
remember a name, that is fine; others can help, or the student can ask the person receiving the toss what it is.

4. To increase the speed of the game, gradually begin to introduce more objects
until 4 to 6 objects are being tossed simultaneously around the circle and multiple students are using each other's names at once.

5. Stop the action. Ask someone to take the challenge of saying every participant's
name. Have members of the group change places in the circle; then have
another person say each name.

6. If you are working with multiple circles, mix them up and do another round
or two until most names have been learned.

Discussion:
None needed.

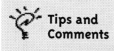
Tips and Comments

- *This can be a good lead-up to the Warp Speed initiative.*
- *This can be played as a warmup on other days to review names in a new group.*

· ·

Chicken Baseball

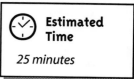
Estimated Time
25 minutes

Setup:
Divide your class into two teams. Teams can range from 5 to 15 or so students.

Framing:
This is an active game that students almost always love. Say to the class, "We're
going to play a game of baseball. This version of baseball has some similarities to
traditional baseball; there are two teams and you can score runs, but that's where
the similarities end."

Check

ut the
daries to
ents and
ove any
stacles.

Emphasize that only one student should be scoring runs at a time; otherwise there could be collisions.

Procedure:

1. One team (team A) is the "infield." The other team (team B) is the "outfield." Team A starts by throwing the rubber chicken anywhere in the designated play area (the entire gym, or a whole soccer field, for example).

2. Once the chicken has been thrown, team B runs toward it and forms a single-file line behind it. The first person in line picks up the chicken and passes it through his or her legs to the person directly behind, who passes it over his or her head. This over-under passing pattern continues until the chicken has reached the end of the line and the last student in line yells, "Stop!"

3. Meanwhile, team A is scoring runs. A run is scored every time one student from team A runs around all of the team A group members. Teams keep track of their own scores, which are cumulative from inning to inning.

4. As soon as team B yells, "Stop," the last student in line throws the chicken to any other spot in the designated play area. Team B then begins to score runs as team A lines up and starts passing the chicken.

5. The game is over after five innings, or when you determine that it's time to stop.

6. If the chicken goes out of bounds (into the bleachers, for example), the team that has thrown it gets to throw again.

Discussion:

Ask students:

- Did each team create strategies that helped them be more successful?
- Did it help that you knew everyone else's name?

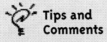

Tips and Comments

- *A rubber chicken really does work best. If you use a ball, it tends to roll and slow the game down.*

- *Add a rule that requires students to choose a different runner to score runs for every inning, so as not to overfatigue the student who is always the last to arrive to the remainder of the team.*

In this lesson, students will experience a sense of community as well as begin to explore similarities and differences.

LESSON 2

Activities
- Card Have You Ever
- Monarch Tag

Lesson Objectives
Students will be able to:

- Experience a sense of community
- Recognize similarities and differences among themselves
- Identify the potential outcomes of cooperative and competitive activities and acceptable attitudes toward both

Materials
- 1 spot marker for each student
- Have You Ever cards, prewritten to be appropriate for your class
- 1 soft foam ball (or 2 if class size is over 20)

ACTIVITIES

Card Have You Ever

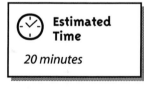

Estimated Time

20 minutes

Setup:
Gather the class in a circle. Place a spot marker at the foot of each person (not including yourself). Add a final spot for yourself (which can be a different color or size), and designate that as the "card-drawing spot."

Framing:
Ask the class, "Have you ever wondered who in this class has traveled to a foreign country, or who speaks another language, or who has more than four siblings?"

Procedure:
1. Ask the first Have You Ever question. Explain to students, "If your answer to the question is yes, then you are to move from your 'home spot' to a new spot, but not the spot next door. If your answer is no, then you are to remain on your home spot. One student will end up on the card-drawing spot. Once everyone is settled, that person will draw a new card and read the next question."

✓ Safety Check

Have students walk to new spots and use "bumpers up." ("Bumpers up" is a technique referred to frequently; it involves students moving with their hands up, palms out, in front of their chests, so that if they collide with anyone, they collide hand to hand, or hand to back.)

2. The person in the card-drawing spot must move to a new spot regardless of whether he or she did or did not answer "yes" to the question. This assures a new person in the card-drawing spot each time.

3. During the activity, you may ask some related follow-up questions to the students who have moved, such as, "What other language do you speak?" or "How many siblings do you have?"

Discussion:

Ask students:

- Were you surprised to see other people move when you did?
- Did you know that you had so many things in common with each other? Did you also know that there were so many differences?

💡 Tips and Comments

- *The activity can be set up with the card-reading spot in the middle. The student who is left without a spot in the circle should stand in the middle and make up his or her own Have You Ever question from personal experience.*

- *Monitor questions for appropriateness, and be sure that the same student does not always end up in the middle.*

- *Card examples: Have you ever?…*
  1. *Been camping?*
  2. *Ridden a subway?*
  3. *Traveled out of state?*
  4. *Traveled out of the country?*
  5. *Been to a concert?*
  6. *Performed in a play?*
  7. *Been in a parade?*
  8. *Sung in a chorus or choir?*
  9. *Played a musical instrument?*
  10. *Been on an athletic team?*
  11. *Volunteered?*

⏱ Estimated Time

30 minutes

Monarch Tag

Setup:

Situate the class in an area with a good amount of running room, but with boundaries. Make sure that the ball or balls that you use are soft and throwable. Remind students that only balls aimed at shoulder level and below are acceptable.

Framing:

Say to students, "In this tag game, we will start with one person who is IT. By the end of the game, everyone will be IT, because everyone will have joined the Monarchy."

Procedure:

1. Select a Monarch—preferably a student with some throwing ability so that the game gets off to a good start. The Monarch (who is IT) is trying to get the Anarchists (the other players) to be Monarchs. The Monarch can do this by hitting other players with the soft foam ball.

2. The designated Monarch starts throwing the ball and trying to hit any of the Anarchists who are running around. Once hit, that Anarchist becomes a Monarch; now the two Monarchs work together to get more Anarchists on their side.

3. A Monarch can only run with the ball when he or she is the only Monarch. After that, only Monarchs who do not have the ball can move. They may pass the ball around to each other. In a class of 20 or more students, we suggest that you start with two Monarchs and two balls.

4. An Anarchist who goes out of bounds automatically turns into a Monarch.

5. The game continues until all of the Anarchists have been "convinced to change their political affiliation" (hit by a ball).

Discussion:

Ask students:

- What parts of this game were competitive? What parts were cooperative?
- How did Monarchs cooperate with each other?
- When Monarchs cooperated, did they get more people to their side?

√ Safety Check

- *Be sure the balls are soft so that students won't mind getting hit.*

- *Have ample running room available, such as in a full-sized gym.*

- *Remind students that a safe, acceptable tag is when the ball hits at or below shoulder level.*

💡 Tips and Comments

• *Add a condition called Royalty Check to the game: Anyone, at any time, can ask for a Royalty Check. This means that all Anarchists have to make a gesture identifying them as Anarchists. Establish this gesture at the start of the game. A good gesture to use is one that looks like the Royal Wave, turning a raised hand at the wrist.*

6.1.3

LESSON 3

This lesson will help students understand the importance of creating a safe environment, will allow them to experiment with cooperative versus competitive behaviors, and will give them opportunities to work together.

Activities
- FFEACH
- Help Me Tag

Lesson Objectives
Students will be able to:
- Work together as a new group
- Understand the importance of creating a safe environment
- Identify possible outcomes of cooperative and competitive behaviors
- Demonstrate positive working relationships with each other

Materials
- 1 or more rubber chickens (for classes over 15, use 2)
- 1-3 soft objects for ITs in Help Me Tag
- List of topics to be used. Examples include Fast Foods, Electrical Appliances, Comic Book Heroes or any other appropriate topics

ACTIVITIES

FFEACH

⏱ **Estimated Time**

30 minutes

Setup:
Divide the class into groups of five to seven people. Separate the groups from each other by a few yards. Situate yourself apart from the groups.

Framing:
Say to students, "In this game you will have a chance to do some speedy charades. You will work with your group to act out as many words as you can in the given time."

Procedure:
Say to students:

1. "In this activity, I will be calling over one member of your group and giving that person a secret topic from one of the following categories: Fast Foods, Electrical Appliances or Comic Book Heroes. A topic might be something like french fries.

2. Your team member will race back to the group and charade that topic until the group guesses it. No talking or writing is allowed.

3. When the team guesses the topic, send another team member to me for another topic to charade.

4. The team in which every member successfully charades a topic first wins."

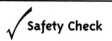

Safety Check

Use common sense in allowing people to "race" back and forth.

Discussion:
None needed.

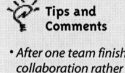

Tips and Comments

• *After one team finishes, allow the others to complete their turns. To stress and incorporate collaboration rather than highlight a winning team, have the team that finishes first join other teams to help them out. This often results in the entire class cheering each other on in delight.*

• *Use any topics that you feel are appropriate for your class. Until you have played this game often, we suggest that you have a list in front of you, as students will be running to you — often in pairs or threes —to get the next topic. You want to be ready!*

• *Have teams come up with a list of topics to be given to the other teams.*

• *Students who are having much difficulty acting out certain words and are getting very frustrated can come back to the teacher for a "refund" (a new topic). Refunds are only issued after a genuine effort has been made to try the original word.*

• *Category and topic examples:*

Fast Foods (FF)	Electrical Appliances (EA)	Comic Book Heroes (CH)
milkshake	microwave	Superman
hamburger	popcorn popper	Batman
french fries	toaster	Pink Panther

$$FF + EA + CH = FFEACH$$

Help Me Tag

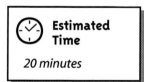

Estimated Time

20 minutes

Setup:
Gather your group so that they can hear your instructions. Set up a boundary that is large enough to allow for some running—about half of a basketball court for 20 students. The area should be flat and free of obstacles.

Framing:
Say to students, "One of the ways in which we can keep each other safe is by understanding how and when to offer each other help. In this tag game, you will

Safety Check

The chicken should be tossed only to students who see that it's coming to them. This helps avoid a chicken in the eye!

have the opportunity to practice giving help and asking for help, all with this rubber chicken!"

Procedure:

1. Select one student to be IT. That student may carry a ball to identify himself or herself. Give the rubber chicken to another student.

2. The person who is IT will try to tag other students. Tags are allowed on the back of the shoulder only.

3. Someone who is about to be tagged can be thrown the rubber chicken before being tagged by IT. Yelling, "Help me! Help me!" is a good way to get the chicken carrier's attention. If this person is tossed the rubber chicken before being tagged by IT, he or she is safe. (People may not be tagged if they are in possession of the chicken.)

4. Any student may handle the rubber chicken except for the person who is IT.

5. If a student is tagged before receiving the rubber chicken, that person becomes the new IT.

Discussion:

Ask students:

- Were you able to ask for help?

- How did your ability to ask for help change when faced with the pressure of being tagged?

- What does asking for help have to do with keeping each other safe?

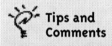 **Tips and Comments**

- For a more challenging variation, add a rule that students may only be tossed the chicken after they have asked for help. In other words, a student who sees that another student needs the chicken may not toss it unless he or she hears "Help me!" This reinforces the skills of asking for help and giving help only when needed.

- For larger classes, add more ITs and more chickens.

This lesson consists of two tag games that are designed to give students a chance to work together as a group. The games should be played only after the class has really begun to take care of each other's safety.

Activities
- Blob Tag
- a.k.a. Tusker Tag

Lesson Objectives
Students will be able to:
- Work together as a new group
- Experience a sense of community

Materials
- 2 boffers (pliable foam swords that cannot cause injury)
- A large space!

ACTIVITIES

Blob Tag

Setup:
This activity should only be done after the group has demonstrated that they are concerned about each other's safety.

Estimated Time
25 minutes

Framing:
Say to students, "This next tag game is one where we really need to take care of each other and make sure that no one gets hurt. I am confident that we are ready to play this, given how well the class has been getting along."

Procedure:
1. Select two people to be IT (the "Blob"), and ask them to link hands or arms. The object of the game is simple; the paired IT group is trying to tag fleeing people. Once someone is tagged, that student joins either end of the Blob and becomes a tagger.
2. Only the end students can tag. The Blob must stay together as one. If the Blob breaks up during the play, any tags that occur then don't count. Any fleeing student who goes outside the boundaries must also join the Blob.

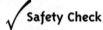
3. The game ends when there is only one person left to be tagged.

Discussion:

Ask students:

- Was the Blob able to stay connected? What helped it work?
- Did the Blob make decisions? Were they good ones?
- Did we take care of each other in this activity?

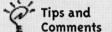

Tips and Comments

Boundaries should not be too big—half of a soccer field for a class of 30 is adequate.

. . . .

Estimated Time

20 minutes

Safety Check

The comments included for Blob Tag also apply here.

a.k.a. Tusker Tag

Setup:
This game can immediately follow Blob Tag.

Framing:
Say to students, "This game is similar to Blob Tag, but this time I would like everyone to pair up and link hands or arms. I will select an IT pair, whose job it will then be to tag another *pair*. Of course, once tagged, that pair joins the IT pair and they become a quartet. The taggers will be given two boffers to use to tag other pairs. "

Procedure:

1. The line of taggers must stay attached; any tags that occur when the line is broken don't count. If a fleeing pair breaks apart, they are automatically caught and required to join the line.
2. The game is over when just one pair is left still free.

Discussion:

Ask students:

- Was it easier or harder to run away when you were paired up or when you were alone, as in Blob Tag?
- How did the line make decisions about where to run? Did you incorporate any learning from Blob Tag?

🔅 Tips and Comments

- *The boffers go to the taggers at each end of the line. As the line gets longer, the boffers are passed to the new taggers at each end. Allow boffer tags to be below the shoulders only.*

- *Allow the line of taggers to "turn around" more quickly by dropping hands, pivoting and regripping hands.*

- *Use a moving boundary: As the tagging line gets longer, discreetly walk backward (designate yourself as a boundary) and enlarge the play area. Students rarely notice and certainly rarely care.*

Section 2: Establishing Full Value Norms

LESSON 1

In this lesson, the group will learn from experience that rules or "ways of being" are needed for them to function successfully and have fun.

Activity
- Pairs Tag

Lesson Objectives
Students will be able to:
- Understand the importance of having a group Full Value Contract

Materials
- Cones for boundaries

ACTIVITY

Pairs Tag

Estimated Time

30 minutes

Setup:
Have everyone pick a partner, or use a pairs activity to help students find partners. Demonstrate "bumpers up" and how it will be used in this activity.

Framing:
Say to students, "When we take time to set up some rules in a game or in a group, it can actually make things more fun."

Procedure:

1. For the first round of this game, there are no physical boundaries set. Ask each pair to pick a song or tune they both know and will use in the game. Go around in a circle and ask each pair to demonstrate its song. Explain to the players that they will be playing tag with just their partners.

2. Ask each pair to choose one player between themselves to be IT. The ITs chase their own partners at a fast walk (no running). When a player who is IT tags his or her partner, the one who has been tagged must spin around once while singing or humming their pair's tune. This person then becomes IT and gets to go after the partner.

3. At the end of the first round, have a brief discussion about the play. Questions might be:

- What worked about this game? What didn't work?
- Did some people go really far away so that their partners didn't have a chance to tag them?
- What would make this a better game, one where everyone has a chance to tag his or her partner?

4. For the second round, establish boundaries for the group. Start with boundaries as large as half of a basketball court. During the play, no one is to step outside these boundary lines. If someone does, the person automatically becomes IT. In subsequent rounds, you can shrink these boundaries, making the game more and more challenging.

Discussion:

Ask students:

- Which way of playing—with boundaries or without boundaries—was more fun?
- Why was the one you chose more fun?
- What was it that made this version of the game work so well?
- How do rules and boundaries help us accomplish things more effectively?

Safety Check

During play, everyone is to use "bumpers up," and everyone must walk.

Tips and Comments

- *As a warmup, have your group practice walking around with their "bumpers up," the goal being not to touch each other.*
- *Although this activity can be done in any space, it is best to have a large, open area either indoors or outdoors.*
- *Simply singing the pair's tune can be an option to turning around and singing.*
- *The first round, with a large space and few boundaries, is meant to spread people out and make it difficult to play.*

LESSON 2

This series of activities will allow the group to experience the five components of a Full Value Contract.

Activities

- Circle Clap
- Pairs Squared
- Fill the Basket
- Asteroids
- Transformer Tag

Lesson Objectives
Students will be able to:

- Learn strategies for personal goal setting
- Understand and recognize actual behaviors that are consistent with the Full Value Contract: Be Here, Be Safe, Set Goals, Be Honest, Let Go and Move On
- Learn strategies for personal goal setting

Materials

- Stopwatch or watch with a secondhand (for Circle Clap)
- Tennis balls and a bucket (for Fill the Basket)
- At least one fleece ball or other soft throwable object for each player (for Asteroids)

ACTIVITIES

Introduce each game with the Full Value Contract component it represents. Include a brief comment about each component's importance for successful group functioning.

Estimated Time

10 minutes

Circle Clap *(Be Here)*

This activity requires full participation and concentration on the part of all group members. It offers a preliminary demonstration of the goal-setting process.

Setup:
Begin with the group in a circle.

Framing:
Introduce the game by telling students that everyone needs to participate fully in order for the group's time to improve.

Procedure:

1. Explain that the object is for the group to pass a single Clap around the circle; this is similar to a Wave being passed around a football stadium. Each person claps once, *immediately* after the preceding person in the circle makes one clap. Determine who will start the CLAP and which way it will go.

2. When the group is ready, say, "Go" and start the timer. At the end of the round, share the time with the group. Ask if they can go faster.

3. Continue with a number of rounds until participants are satisfied with the time.

. . . .

Pairs Squared *(Be Safe)*

This is an active walking activity.

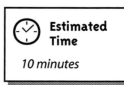

Estimated Time

10 minutes

Setup:

Have everyone pick a partner, or use a pairs activity to help students find partners.

Framing:

Introduce the game by telling participants that it is important to have a safe environment for members of a group. Each member contributes to creating this sense of safety. Remind them that they particularly need to be aware of their partners during the play, since they will be linked together. "Bumpers up" will be used in this activity.

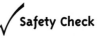

√ **Safety Check**

- *Students must use "bumpers up" and must walk only.*
- *Have players check in with each other to be aware of each other's needs.*
- *Pairs may not go between people who are linked (other pairs).*

Procedure:

1. This game is played in nearly the same way as Pairs Tag in Grade 6, Section 2, Lesson 1. However, this time players start off in pairs, either holding hands or locking arms. The other rules are the same.

2. One pair is IT and is trying to tag its partner pair. When a pair gets tagged, it must spin around twice, humming a tune, before becoming IT and starting to chase its paired partner.

3. Partners must "be safe" and not drag each other around the floor.

. . . .

Fill the Basket *(Set Goals)*

This activity focuses on throwing skills. It also requires the group to determine strategies and roles in their approach to the challenge. In this game, the group sets a goal for itself: how many balls it will be able to get into the bucket in a two-minute time period.

Estimated Time

30 minutes

Setup:

Place a bucket in the center of a designated play area. A good playing area is half of a regular gym. Lines on the gymnasium floor, rope or cones should mark the boundaries for the throwers. Have players stand outside the boundaries. Place the balls, also outside the boundaries, in front of the players.

Framing:

Introduce the game by discussing the idea that realistic goals are important for a group to have so that it can monitor its progress. Everyone must be included in one role or another so that every member feels a part of a team; this enhances the whole group's effort.

Procedure:

1. The object of this game is to have the group get as many tennis balls as possible into the bucket in a two-minute time period. There are two types of players: the throwers and the retrievers. The class decides how many throwers and how many retrievers they will have for each round. The throwers must remain behind the boundaries. The retrievers may stand in any place they wish, but they may not "help" the balls into the bucket in any way. Their job is simply to retrieve missed shots and roll the balls back to the throwers as quickly as possible. Players may not change positions during a round. (Other rules allow "helping," but requiring the retrievers to use their hands only to get the balls back to the throwers leads to more interesting game strategies.)

2. At the end of each round, allow players to make any adjustments to their positions, and let teams discuss changing their tactics.

3. Continue with rounds until the goal is achieved or time runs out. If it seems that the group has set an unrealistic goal, ask if they would like to reconsider their goal and set a new one.

Asteroids *(Be Honest)*

This activity can be a very active running game. It is a self-elimination game.

Setup:

Begin by giving one fleece ball to each of the players. Have group members spread themselves out within the defined playing area.

Framing:

Introduce this game by reminding the group that honesty is crucial for a safe environment that allows members to take risks. This involves being honest with others as well as with oneself.

Procedure:

1. At a designated signal, players start tossing their balls into the air and allowing them to hit the ground. The play then begins with each player picking up any ball from the floor and throwing it, attempting to hit another player *below the waist.*

2. Once hit, a player stoops down and is out. If a ball is in the player's hand when he or she is hit, that ball must be rolled away.

3. The round ends when there is only one player left standing.

4. For a second round, if a ball rolls by a squatting player who can reach it, that player can take the ball, get back up, and resume playing.

. . . .

Transformer Tag (Let Go and Move On)

This activity can be a very active running game, or you may set rules that restrict it to walking.

Setup:
This game can immediately follow Asteroids.

Framing:
Introduce this game by reminding the group that the ability to proceed with any task at hand by putting aside differences and moving forward is critical to accomplishing that task. In this game, players regularly change teams, let go of their connections to one side and join their opponents.

Procedure:
1. Show the group the two body positions they will be using in this game: one hand on top of the head, or one hand behind the back. Ask each person to choose one of these positions, but tell them not to do it yet.

2. Explain that as soon as everyone is ready, you will begin the game by yelling, "Transform!" Each player will take his or her selected position. Those with hands on their heads will try to tag those with hands behind their backs, and vice versa. If tagged, a player then "transforms" to the other position and begins trying to tag former teammates.

3. Play continues until everyone is on one team and there is no one left to tag.

4. Have rematches as time and interest allow, pointing out that group members may change their starting positions for each match.

Discussion:
At the end of each of the games, ask the group for specific examples of how the Full Value Contract component being addressed was a part of the game. Ask, "Who can explain, from this game or from your own experience, how 'Being Here' is important for our Full Value Contract?" (Change Being Here to Setting Goals, etc., depending on the activity.)

Estimated Time

15 minutes

Safety Check

Remind the class about what constitutes an appropriate tag.

Tips and Comments

At the end of each activity, you may want to record on a flipchart or whiteboard the students' comments about the Full Value component being addressed. You can then incorporate these comments into the next activity, Feelings Marketplace Cards.

LESSON 3

Doing Adventure activities evokes many different thoughts and feelings. It is good for participants to be able to recognize and identify them. The activity in this lesson will help the group identify the feelings that accompany Full Value Contract behaviors.

Activity
- Marketplace Relay

Lesson Objectives
Students will be able to:
- Identify respectful behaviors toward self, peers and adults.
- Develop the group's Full Value Contract

Materials
- Set of Feelings Marketplace Cards

ACTIVITY

Marketplace Relay

Estimated Time

20 minutes

Setup:
Choose cards from the set of Feelings Marketplace Cards that are appropriate for the group doing this activity. Divide the group into teams of four or five players each. Have the teams stand at an equal distance from you, similar to the setup of FFEACH (Grade 6, Section 1, Lesson 3)

Framing:
Say to students, "We all have a range of feelings. This activity helps us to identify many different types of feelings and helps us express those feelings to others."

Procedure:
1. This is an active game of charades in which players act out words from the Feelings cards. Each player will be shown a card and will then help his or her team discover the word by acting out the feeling—no talking allowed for the actor. The first group to guess all of its words wins.
2. When everyone is ready, say, "Go." One person from each team runs to you and gets a card. The person reads the card, leaving it on the floor by your feet. The person must then run back and act out the feeling for his or her team. Once a team guesses the feeling correctly, a new player from that group can come to you to get a new card.

3. The relay continues until one of the teams has either successfully guessed five feelings or until each person's card has been guessed (you will decide which of these limits works best for your group).

Safety Check

No special safety procedures required for this activity.

Discussion:

- Have the teams pick cards that describe feelings associated with the Full Value Contract concepts. (See Introduction for Cornerstones of an Adventure Program.)

- On a large sheet of paper or a whiteboard, write these words under the appropriate Full Value heading. When finished, have the group look at all the words that describe the FVC concepts. Ask if there are any other words they would like to add to their lists.

- Discuss how these behaviors, if appropriately adopted, show respect for self and others.

 **Tips and Comments**

- *If a group gets really stuck on a word or the person acting does not know what the word is, pull that card out and substitute a new one. You may want to have students create a symbol for their FVC, or have them sign the list of feelings that they have created in this lesson, so that they all feel committed to the contract.*

- *Any student who is having real trouble acting out a word can ask for a "refund" and get another. Refunds are only given after the student has genuinely tried the original word.*

LESSON 4

Now that the group has a Full Value Contract, it is important to try it out. This lesson is an activity that involves applying the concepts worked on in the past lessons to a fun game. At the end, students will reflect on how well they are using Full Value concepts in the group.

Activity
- Warp Speed

Lesson Objectives
Students will be able to:

- Identify techniques for maintaining the Full Value Contract
- Understand that the Full Value Contract can be used effectively to manage conflict within the group
- Understand and recognize behaviors that are consistent with the FVC

Materials

- Soft, throwable object such as a rubber chicken to be passed/tossed around the circle. Have more objects on hand to add in if appropriate—see Tips and Comments.
- A stopwatch

ACTIVITY

Warp Speed

Estimated Time

30 minutes

Setup:
Arrange your group in a circle.

Framing:
In this activity, students will use problem-solving and listening skills to work together to accomplish the task. It is generally sufficient to begin by telling the group that they will need to work together to solve a problem, while increasing the speed with which they accomplish the task. Alternative framing could be to tell them that the object they are passing represents a goal that they need to accomplish as a group.

Procedure:

1. Begin by explaining that each person, in turn, is going to receive an object and then toss it to someone else (who hasn't previously received it). The last person

who receives it will return the object to you to complete the cycle. Be certain to tell players that they must remember who throws the object to them and to whom they throw it. If everyone remembers correctly, the group established a pattern in which each person catches the ball from one particular person and tosses it to another.

Rules:

- Passing of the object must start and stop with the same person (whoever starts it must get it back to complete the cycle).
- The object must move sequentially from person to person (not everyone can touch it at the same time).
- Each player must have possession of the object as it moves through the cycle.

2. After establishing a baseline time for completing the cycle and pattern with the object, ask the group how it can get faster and faster each time.

Discussion:

Ask students:

- How did we do on the Full Value Contract concepts we have been talking about?
- Which of them are working well for this group?
- Which ones need more work?
- Do we need to add any more concepts to our list?

Tips and Comments

- *Allow the group to try many different options, including breaking out of the circle.*
- *This is a great all-purpose problem-solving initiative. Depending on the skill level of the group, you can introduce more than one object into what must be passed sequentially. Introducing an egg as one of the objects to be passed adds an interesting dynamic to the problem-solving process.*
- *If you have a group of more than 15, consider breaking the large group into smaller teams. Each small group will simultaneously accomplish the task. Debrief first in the smaller groups before joining the groups into one.*

ASSESSMENT OPTION

A student's knowledge of his or her own self-esteem can be very enlightening. Adventure activities often bring self-esteem issues to light. Use the Self-Esteem Self-Assessment tool provided in the Assessment section at the end of this book to give students an opportunity to evaluate their own individual levels of self-esteem. This tool can be used again later in the curriculum to assess whether there have been any significant changes.

✓ **Safety Check**

No special safety procedures required for this activity.

Section 3: Problem Solving

LESSON 1

In this lesson, students will do their first problem-solving activity. This is a fun initiative that involves some physical skill as well as total group participation.

Activity

- Turnstile

Lesson Objectives

Students will be able to:

- Identify the different strengths of individuals in the group
- Work together to achieve a common goal
- Learn techniques to solve problems to accomplish group tasks
- Understand the importance of contributing ideas in the process of solving problems

Materials

- Jumping rope about 50' long

ACTIVITY

Turnstile

Estimated Time

30 minutes

Setup:

Select an additional rope turner to assist you. Ask the rest of the class to stand on one side of the jump rope. Begin turning.

Framing:

Say to students, "This activity requires that the entire group participate both in solving the problem and in implementing the solution. The task is simple: Everyone must get through the turning rope. Once the group begins going through, the jumping area can never be empty again."

Procedure:

Rules are:

- One person at a time
- Pass (jump, run) through without touching the rope
- No missing a beat (the rope can't turn without a jumper jumping)
- The initiative continues until the entire group has gone through the rope. If a rule is broken, the entire group begins again.

Safety Check

If someone hits the rope, stop turning or you may cause the student to trip or fall.

Discussion:

Ask students:

- Was the group successful? Why?
- How were ideas shared?
- What helped you get organized enough to succeed?
- Did you discover different strengths amongst your teammates? Name some.

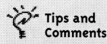

Tips and Comments

- *Depending on students' skill level, you can have them do some easier lead-up activities, such as running through the turning rope without jumping.*
- *Turn the rope toward the person who is entering the arc. This is much easier for the runner.*

6.3.2

LESSON 2

This is a good time to introduce or review the ABCDEs of Problem Solving. It provides the class with a tool to help them improve their group problem-solving process. This lesson offers an entertaining, active problem to solve.

Activity
- Don't Touch Me

Lesson Objectives
Students will be able to:
- Work together to achieve a common goal
- Learn techniques to solve problems to accomplish group tasks
- Understand the importance of contributing ideas in the process of solving problems

Materials
- 1 Hula Hoop™
- Flipchart (if needed) for the ABCDEs of Problem Solving

. . . .

ACTIVITY

Estimated Time

30 minutes

Don't Touch Me

Setup:
Place the Hula Hoop™ on the ground. Creatively split the class into two even groups, one on each side of the hoop. With classes over 24, you may want to use 4 groups.

Review or teach the ABCDEs of Problem Solving:

Ask questions to understand the problem.
Brainstorm solutions openly.
Choose a solution to implement.
Do it.
Evaluate the solution, adopt or discard it, and repeat this process again if needed.

Framing:
Say to students, "We learned some things about how we can be organized to solve a group problem during Turnstile. Here is another initiative that will also require

the class to be organized. Today each of you will be 'on center stage' for just a moment. This is how it works…"

Procedure:

1. Each group needs to get to the other side of the hoop as quickly as possible.
2. While changing sides, some body part must touch inside the hoop.
3. There can be no physical contact with anyone during the activity.
4. Any rule infraction results in a three-second penalty added to the group's final time.
5. When more than one person is in the hoop, these players must simultaneously yell, "Don't touch me!" All players need to remember to keep "bumpers up."
6. Have the group go through one trial round. Then allow them 15–20 minutes to set a "world record time." If you want to emphasize goal setting, have them agree upon the desired group time after the trial.

Discussion:

Ask students:

- What learning did you apply from the last initiative? Did it help?
- If not, how did the group improve on their time?
- Were different ideas accepted and heard?
- How did you select a particular idea?
- Do we need to add anything to our Full Value Contract?

> **√ Safety Check**
>
> • *Remind students of bumper's up when running through the hoop.*
>
> • *Make sure that the ground is clear and level.*

LESSON 3

This lesson offers a nice contrast to the previous lesson. Rather than having students attempt to move about while making <u>no</u> contact with others, this lesson asks the group to move around <u>while</u> making contact. Once again, the group is posed with a unique problem to solve.

Activity
- Welded Ankles

Lesson Objectives
Students will be able to:
- Work together to achieve a common goal
- Learn procedures that are safe and effective for the given task
- Understand the importance of contributing ideas in the process of solving problems
- Understand techniques to evaluate the process of problem solving

Materials
- Boundary ropes

ACTIVITY

Estimated Time
30 minutes

Welded Ankles

Setup:
Place 2 boundary lines about 15 feet apart. Ask the class to split into groups of about 15. This activity can be done in smaller or larger groups, the difficulty increasing as the group gets larger.

Framing:
Say to students, "This activity will require you to follow a variety of different directions, both in small groups and as a whole class. You are all working together to achieve the same goals, so feel free to assist each other if needed."

Procedure:
1. Have students move in their groups across the playing area. Everyone within a group must be touching hands with the next person. Contact must be maintained throughout the move from one boundary line to the opposite one.
2. Have groups move across the play area while touching shoulders.

3. Next, have groups move across the play area while touching hips.

4. Then, have groups move across the play area while touching ankles. Contact still needs to be maintained at all times while crossing the area.

Students may not tie their waists or ankles together. When one group has finished, it can disperse and help the others.

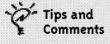

Safety Check

Be careful not to allow groups to tie themselves together.

Discussion:

Have students form the small groups they were in at the beginning of this activity for the following discussion:

- Did your group effectively use the ABCDEs of Problem Solving?
- Which stage of the problem-solving model did your group do best (A, B, C, D, E)?
- Was it easier to do this activity in a smaller group than it would have been if I had asked the entire class to do the activity as one group? Why?
- Did you help, or get help from, others in the class?
- What contributed to meeting the common goal?
- Was it important to have many different ideas contributed?
- Pick one key idea or thing you have learned to share with the rest of the class.

Tips and Comments

- You can start with even smaller groups of two to four students for an easier progression. (Remember, adding people to a group makes this activity much more challenging!)

- If working with very small groups, increase the distance that they must travel.

- It is best to start with smaller groups, then work up to larger groups of about 15, for the "welded ankles" version of the activity.

LESSON 4

This lesson helps students learn how to negotiate with other groups. Be prepared with additional activities, as this one can take just a few minutes—or a very long time!

Activity

- Negotiation Square

Lesson Objectives
Students will be able to:

- Work together to achieve a common goal
- Identify and practice both followership and leadership in accomplishing group tasks

Materials
None needed

ACTIVITY

Negotiation Square

Estimated Time

20 minutes

Setup:
Have the class break into four equal groups. They should stand so that the groups form the four points of a square. Each group should face the group on the opposite side of the square.

Framing:
Say to students, "This activity will test your powers of negotiation and psychic energy!"

Procedure:

1. Ask each group to step away from the square and, privately, to create a motion accompanied by a sound that will represent their group. *The motion and sound need to be easily learned and repeated by others.*

2. Ask the groups to come back to the square. One at a time, each group should demonstrate their motion and sound. Ask the other groups to learn and practice each motion and sound that is presented

3. Ask each group to once again step away from the square. The groups must now decide on one of the four motions and sounds they have learned that they will

do next. *The goal of the activity is, without planning or communicating with the other groups, for the entire class to do the same motion and sound simultaneously!*

4. When each group has decided quietly what they are going to do, have the square come back together. On the count of three, everyone does their motion.

5. In rare instances, the whole class will do the same motion the first time. If not, have the groups continue the activity until the class all performs the same motion.

6. Observe how the class does or does not negotiate. Remember, groups may not talk to each other!

Discussion:

Ask students:

- *(Each group should briefly discuss the following, then share as a whole class.)* What did you feel were positive actions by the other groups? What did you feel were negative actions by the other groups?

- Did the class manage to negotiate easily? Why or why not?

- Was it hard to not do your own motion? Did you feel that you were giving up too much by doing another group's motion and sound?

- What made you all finally get it? Was it just luck?

- What can we learn from this about negotiating with other groups in school, or with others in this class?

- What kinds of leadership emerged? How about followership? Why are both important?

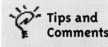

Tips and Comments

- If the class arrives at the same sound and motion in the first round or so, do the activity again with new groups, new motions and new sounds!

- If it takes groups awhile to coordinate, observe their frustration and intervene only if necessary. They do eventually get it, so be patient.

> ✓ **Safety Check**
>
> *No special safety procedures required for this activity.*

6.3.5

LESSON 5

Continuing to apply the ABCDEs of problem solving, students are asked in this lesson to cross an area of the gym or field without touching the ground. Resource management and communication become critical in this activity.

Activity
- Stepping Stones

Lesson Objectives
Students will be able to:
- Work together to achieve a common goal
- Identify and practice both leadership and followership in accomplishing group tasks
- Learn procedures that are safe and effective for the given task
- Understand techniques to evaluate the process of solving problems
- Learn positive mechanisms to deal with failure

Materials
- Foam stepping-stone blocks, one per student
- Masking tape and markers
- Short boundary markers

ACTIVITY

Stepping Stones

Estimated Time

30 minutes

Setup:
The class can do this as one group if there are no more than 20 students. If there are more than 20, divide the class in two. Mark a distance that the group(s) must travel; this distance should be a few more paces than the number of students in one group. With boundary markers, mark the beginning and the end of the distance to be covered. If you are working with more than one group, ask each group to stand behind opposite boundary markers.

Framing:
1. Explain to the class that they have already effectively solved many problems. Ask each of them to take a minute and think of a positive quality that has helped the class be successful. Have each class member write a chosen quality on a piece of tape and attach it to his or her stepping stone. They should then report out to the class.

2. Say to students, "You are all part of a special unit that is being given a very

difficult mission." (If there are two or more groups, emphasize that every group is part of the same special unit.) "Your mission is to cross this very toxic area designated by these boundary ropes. Your goal is for the entire special unit to be successful."

Procedure:

1. Every member of each group must get across the marked area, from one boundary line to the other.

2. No one may touch the ground; participants can only stand on the foam stones.

3. Players must remain in contact with the stones *at all times*. If a stone is left unattended for any period of time, that resource, or "quality," is lost. Tell students, "Remember, we must stay attentive to the qualities that have made us successful."

4. If any group member touches the ground for any reason, then the entire class must go back to the start.

Discussion:

- Have each group meet to list the qualities that were most present during their mission.

- Have each group report out to the class, giving examples of when these qualities were most present.

- If the class was not successful, have each group analyze which qualities were missing to prevent success.

- Have each participant consider individually which quality he or she exhibited most often as part of the team.

- Ask students to think about how they dealt with failure or frustration. What have they learned?

Safety Check

- *If you are using something other than the foam squares, be careful that the "stones" you're using are not too slippery.*

- *Do not allow students to carry each other.*

- *Be careful to ensure that students do not jump too far to a boundary line.*

Tips and Comments

- *Stones (qualities) can be given back to the class if you, as facilitator, observe that a particular quality is really present.*

- *Another technique to consider trying is: if a quality is "lost," ask the group to identify some techniques or behaviors they could practice that would help them get the quality back. Award a positive brainstorm with a reissue of that quality.*

- *If there are two groups, allow them to share resources. This is important to allow so that they understand they are working as one unit, rather than competing with each other*

ASSESSMENT OPTION

Evaluate the class's problem-solving ability using the Problem Solving—Group Assessment Checklist provided in the Assessment section near the back of this book. You can use this either to assess all of the problem-solving lessons or simply to assess this individual lesson.

Section 4: Building Trust

LESSON 1

This lesson will stimulate some discussions about trust and will prepare the class for additional trust activities in Lesson 2. Students will have opportunities to practice respecting each other for making different decisions.

Activities
- Challenge Circles
- Velcro Circle

Lesson Objectives
Students will be able to:
- Understand the importance of respecting and supporting their own and other students' decisions regarding personal level of challenge.
- Identify reliable behaviors that offer physical and emotional support
- Understand the value of expressing their feelings in a supportive environment

Materials
- Play ropes of various lengths

ACTIVITIES

Challenge Circles

Estimated Time
15 minutes

Setup:
Use the play ropes to create two concentric circles on the ground. There should be about four feet between each of the rope circles. The inner circle should be large enough so that the entire class could stand inside. Circle the whole group up around the outer circle. Show students that the inner circle represents one's comfort zone, the middle circle one's stretch zone and the outer circle the panic zone, which can extend out quite far.

Framing:
Say to the class, "We've been practicing Challenge by Choice. Can someone review what that means?" Remind students, "Everyone has a comfort zone, a stretch zone and a panic zone; Challenge by Choice says that you should try to stay in your

stretch zone. But, does everyone have the same comfort zone, the same stretch zone and the same panic zone?"

Procedure:

1. Review the differences between a comfort zone, a stretch zone and a panic zone. Give some examples of each: "A comfort zone is where you are comfortable—maybe on the bus with friends, maybe at a birthday party. A stretch zone is where you are not entirely comfortable, but you're not panicked—you're in your 'zone.' The panic zone is where you feel a lot of anxiety, and all you want to do is get right back into your comfort zone."

2. Explain to the class that you are going to call out a topic—perhaps snakes, or cooking.

3. Students are to go to the zone where that topic puts them. (For example, do snakes put them in their comfort zone, stretch zone or panic zone?)

4. Do not overexplain each topic; allow students to interpret them as they wish.

5. After each round, have students look around and notice the diversity of responses.

Discussion:

Ask students:

- Did people usually end up in different places? What does that mean about this class?

- How is the Full Value Contract an important part of our having all of these differences?

- What does it mean when someone chooses to participate in a way that is different from others?

· ·

Velcro Circle

Setup:

Gather the class together for the instructions. Make sure that you have a large play field and that it is clear of any obstacles.

Framing:

Say to students, "In this activity, you will have the opportunity to take into account the three different comfort zones, and you will help keep each other safe."

Procedure:

1. Gather the group into a "Velcro circle"—a circle so tight that if students had Velcro on their shoulders, they would stick together.

> **√ Safety Check**
>
> • *Be sure that the class is ready to do this "eyes shut" activity. It is important to know that they will stop when you ask them.*
>
> • *Remind students to muddle slowly so as not to run into anyone else or any other objects.*

2. Explain that each player is to have a conversation with both of his or her immediate neighbors. The conversation begins with the question, "How are you doing?" The response is always, "Just fine, thanks." This conversation should go on until everyone has asked and responded several times.

3. Explain that *muddling* is a special walk that students will have a chance to do. Muddling is how penguins walk, with their feet close together and their "hands" (wings) up in front of them.

4. Ask students to close their eyes. Remind them of their responsibility to take care of themselves—in this case, to peek—f they are in their panic zone.

5. Instruct students to turn out from the circle, with their eyes closed, and to muddle until you yell, "Stop!"

6. Students will muddle about and scatter. Monitor everyone for safety (muddling will keep them from walking too fast).

7. Yell, "Stop!" and inform students that the next challenge is to reform exactly their original circle—still keeping their eyes closed. Their only method of identifying their original neighbors in the circle is by using the phrases: "How are you doing?" and "Just fine, thanks."

8. Students may open their eyes when the whole group believes that everyone is in the right place.

Discussion:

• How did it feel to have your eyes closed at the same time as everyone else?

• What helped you get back into your original circle? Did everyone use the same strategies, or did players have different strategies that helped toward the goal?

• Did people practice Challenge by Choice?

• Did the class create a supportive environment?

• Do you feel comfortable expressing your feelings in the environment that this class has created?

Tips and Comments

If the class is larger than 25, consider doing the first round in two groups and a second round with the entire class.

This lesson continues to focus on trust. Students will have opportunities to experience trust, to experience a potential lack of trust, and to articulate their ideas on what trust entails.

6.4.2

LESSON 2

Activities
- Bumper Cars
- Trust Wave

Lesson Objectives
Students will be able to:

- Understand the concept of CBC (Challenge by Choice) in regard to risk-taking situations

- Understand that progressive personal challenges, taken on in a safe environment, can lead to increased self-awareness and learning opportunities

- Identify reliable behaviors that offer physical and emotional support to others

Materials
- Cones or a boundary rope

ACTIVITIES

Bumper Cars

Setup:
Ask the class to break into pairs. Create a boundary, using cones or a long rope, that will force the pairs to have to move around each other during the activity.

Framing:
Ask students, "Have you ever driven a car? Would you like to? This activity will give you a chance to drive a car. You will need to keep the car very safe, which means you are not going to crash into any other cars or any obstacles."

Procedure:
1. Each pair selects who will be the "car" and who will be the "driver." The car will keep his or her eyes closed while being driven around.

Estimated Time
20 minutes

Safety Check

• *Be sure that the group is ready for this activity —in other words, that they have established a caring environment.*

• *Bumpers up!*

• *Ask all drivers not to drive too fast.*

2. The driver's goal is to drive around without any crashes. Because cars don't talk, no talking is allowed! The signals that the driver can use are: both hands on the shoulder of the car to go forward, both hands off to stop, tap the right shoulder to turn right, tap the left shoulder to turn left, and tap both shoulders to go in reverse.

3. Give each driver about two minutes of driving time, and then have partners switch roles.

Discussion:

Ask students:

• Did you like being the driver or the car the most? (Share this with your partner.) Why?

• [As a large group] Did the driver keep you safe? How?

• What are some things that we can do to help people trust us?

Tips and Comments

You can add restrictions by placing signs on the floor that drivers need to follow, such as "One Way" or "U Turn."

Estimated Time

25 minutes

Trust Wave

Setup:

Ask the class to form two lines that face each other. The distance between the two lines should be enough so that opposing players stand wrist to wrist if they were to extend their arms out in front of them.

Framing:

Say to students, "Have you ever done the Wave at a sporting event? Why does a crowd do the Wave? Yes, to cheer their team on. In this activity, you will be doing a Wave as you cheer on your classmates. You will also be the "spotters" for this activity. The object of the activity is for one person—the "runner"—to walk, jog or run all the way down between the two lines. Each participant will select his or her own level of challenge in this activity, so remember the Challenge by Choice philosophy."

Procedure:

1. Select a volunteer to be the runner. This player should start about 10 yards from the head of the two lines. Establish a communication system like the one used during the Trust Fall: The runner yells, "Ready?" He or she does not start until the group responds, "Ready." The runner then yells, "Running." The group responds, "Run." Now the runner can begin.

2. The runner, using whatever pace is comfortable, approaches the lines *maintaining the same speed throughout the run or walk*. The spotters (all of the people in the two lines) are positioned with their arms outstretched, heads turned toward the runner. As the runner approaches them, and just before it is too late, each pair of spotters raise their arms up so that the runner passes untouched. This motion looks like a giant wave as it passes down the double line.

3. Allow the runner a second turn to increase his or her speed.

4. Allow any other student who would like to be the runner to do so.

Discussion:

Ask students:

- Were you able to trust that the spotters would move in time? Why?

- Were you able to go faster on your second try?

- Would anyone who chose not to go like to share why?

- Is trust something that can be gained and lost?

Safety Check

- *Make sure that each runner starts far enough away for the group to be able to judge the runner's speed.*

- *With more than 12 people in a line, make sure that everyone is paying attention and can see the runner coming.*

- *Use even ground.*

- *Use clear commands.*

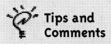
Tips and Comments

- *Keep this activity moving. It can get long for the spotters if they don't get to have a turn. The activity looks easier than it is for the runner!*

- *Each runner, in addition to choosing the pace, can also ask the group for a sound effect that the runner should make for the group while running down the line.*

Section 5: Experiences Using Low Elements

LESSON 1

This lesson gives the class an opportunity to truly work together. Students will literally be connected as they move across an area. Respecting differences and having compassion for each other as they move through the activity is important.

Activities
- Balloon Trolleys
- Trolleys

Lesson Objectives
Students will be able to:

- Physically challenge themselves in a safe environment
- Understand their own strengths and weaknesses

Materials
- Balloons or beach balls, one per student
- A cone or other marker for each group
- Sets of trolleys (obtainable through Project Adventure) so there are enough ropes or positions for each member of the class
- Objects (equaling the number of students in the class) to be picked up along the trolley route. Rubber chickens, soft foam balls and other soft objects are all examples of appropriate items.

ACTIVITY

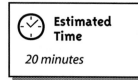

Estimated Time

20 minutes

Balloon Trolleys

Setup:
Divide the class into groups of about 10 to 12 each.

Framing:
Say to students, "This activity is the first stage of training for your lunar research trip. To prepare for walking on the moon trolleys, we first need to practice walking as a group."

Procedure:

1. Have each group of students stand in single file.

2. Place a balloon or beach ball between each student so that the ball is being held up between a student's back and another student's torso.

3. Explain to each group that their task is to move together as a group without dropping any of the balls.

4. If a ball is dropped, assign an appropriate penalty—from going back by three feet to starting over again. This will depend on individual class abilities and how much success you want them to have.

5. Students must keep their hands on their own shoulders and avoid touching the balloon or ball with their hands.

6. The goal is for each group to move to a designated distance about 15 feet away, then to go around a cone (or other marker) and head back to the starting place without dropping any of the balls or balloons.

Safety Check

• *Make sure that the area of play is clear of obstacles.*

• *Allergies to latex are quite prevalent; when in doubt, use beach balls.*

Discussion:

Ask the class:

• What do we need to remember about traveling as a group?

• What makes it easier? What makes it more difficult?

Tips and Comments

Both distance and the addition of turns in the travel path affect the difficulty of this activity.

Trolleys

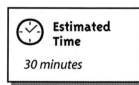
Estimated Time

30 minutes

Setup:

Divide the class into the correct number of groups so that each student will have a position and a rope on a trolley.

Framing:

Say to students, "You have been brought to the moon to do some research. Because of the extremely difficult terrain and environment, there is only one way for you to travel across the research area: you must use the trolleys that I am providing you. The entire class, which really means every scientist, must go on the journey. Each of you must collect an item along the way, which represents the data that you are collecting. In order for the data to be relevant, the entire class must get to the other end of the research area."

Procedure:

1. No one is allowed to touch the ground. Penalties for this can vary depending on the ability of the group—everyone must go back, only that one trolley group must go back, everyone goes back 10 feet, everyone must change positions on the trolley, etc.

2. No one is allowed to tie feet or hands to the trolley or trolley handles.

3. Anyone who feels as if he or she is going to fall should preferably step off before causing others to fall, too.

4. Objects must be picked up along the way by each member of the research team.

5. If split into multiple groups, the class can either be briefed as one research team all working together, or as multiple teams trying to collect their own groups of data. The dynamics of the class will certainly differ depending on which option you choose.

Discussion:

Ask the students:

• How did group members communicate with each other? Did being in a line challenge your communication? How?

• Did individuals help others? How? What did that look like?

• Did everyone retrieve an item?

• Were you competitive or collaborative with the other groups?

• How were individuals who needed to step off treated?

 **Tips and Comments**

Remember Challenge by Choice! If there are students who are uncomfortable being on a trolley, ask them to be observers of the class's process.

This lesson offers additional opportunities for creative problem solving. Differences in individual abilities can be addressed and supported while students successfully complete the activity.

6.5.2

LESSON 2

Activity

• TP Shuffle

Lesson Objectives

Students will be able to:

• Physically challenge themselves in a safe environment

• Understand their own strengths and weaknesses

• Understand the value of relying on their group to support positive risk taking

Materials

• TP Shuffle low element (log or telephone pole), obtainable through Project Adventure

ACTIVITY

TP Shuffle

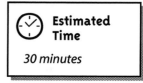

Estimated Time

30 minutes

Setup:

Split the class into two groups. One group should be lined up near each end of the log.

Framing:

Say to the class, "Each of you is a member of a group that has just reached a peaceful solution to a conflict. To acknowledge and confirm this agreement, each group must stand on the log and change ends with the other group. When passing someone from the other group, you must acknowledge him or her in a special way. You must all agree on what that special acknowledgment will be."

Procedure:

1. No one is allowed to step off the log, not even when passing members of the other group.

2. Advise anyone who is about to fall off to *step off* before causing anyone else to fall, too.

✓ **Safety Check**

- *Make sure that the log or pole is appropriate for this activity.*

- *Wet logs are more slippery.*

- *Check around the log for any obstacles on the ground—bees' nests, sticks, rocks, etc.*

- *Remind students to step off the log before they fall off.*

- *Do not allow running or jumping on the log*

3. Remind students, "I am the only spotter here, so please do not push anyone or be careless on the log."

Discussion:

Ask students:

- Did you apply any of what you learned about communicating in a line from the Trolleys activity to this activity? How?

- Were you able to support the differences that exist in the group? What were some of the differences, and how did you support them?

- Was the entire group safe? What helped create this safe environment?

Tips and Comments

- *This can also be done as a line-up activity: Ask everyone to stand on the log. Once they are all up, then ask students to rearrange the line according to something like birthdays, etc.*

- *This activity can be done more than once, allowing the class to perfect their technique.*

- *After the class has tried a few crossing methods, ask them to pick some of their favorites. Then challenge them to do the activity a few more times, but in each round using only one of these crossing methods.*

ASSESSMENT OPTION

Supporting differences has been a theme throughout this unit. Class discussions are a difficult way to evaluate each student's progress around the issue of respecting differences. Use the Respect for Differences—Journal Questions tool (provided in the Assessment section near the end of this book) to gain a better understanding of individual student progress in this area.

This lesson is a great final challenge for the sixth grade. Problem solving, taking care of each other and having fun are all incorporated.

LESSON 3

Activity
- Nitro Crossing

Lesson Objectives

Students will be able to:

- Physically challenge themselves in a safe environment
- Understand their own strengths and weaknesses
- Understand the importance of respecting other's strengths and weaknesses
- Understand the value of relying on their group to support positive risk taking
- Identify how fatigue affects performance and can lead to injury
- Demonstrate proper spotting techniques

Materials
- Swing rope, obtainable through Project Adventure
- Boundary markers or very low bar for the start of the activity
- Bucket filled nearly to the top with water

ACTIVITY

Nitro Crossing

Setup:

1. Properly hang the swing rope. Set the swing boundaries according to the ability of the class. The far boundary line designates where the "island" begins in this activity story line.

2. You may use a very short bar at the start area for students to swing over. Make sure that the bar will easily fall if hit and that it is less than a foot off the ground.

3. Fill a bucket nearly full with water, or use a bucket of balls.

Framing:

Say to the class, "You are a group of doctors who have been brought in to deliver much-needed medicine to the people on this island. The medicine is in this bucket and cannot be spilled. If any is spilled, the entire mixture becomes ineffective,

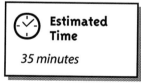

Estimated Time

35 minutes

so you will all have to return to the start and refill it. Everyone—and the medicine—must get on the island by swinging across on this rope."

Procedure:

1. No one is allowed to touch the area between the start and the "island."
2. No water or balls can be spilled.
3. Everyone must start over if either of the above happens.
4. The rope will start in the middle of the area!
5. Make sure that people are spotted at the start and finish of their swings.
6. When students let go with their arms, they need to make sure that their feet are out of the loop on the rope.
7. The swinger must communicate with spotters and with the people who have already made it to the island before swinging.
8. No wild swinging.

Discussion:

Ask students:

• Did everyone agree on the initial solution to this problem? If not, did you feel OK about saying so?

• How did you select the person who took the water across? Did anyone feel left out in that process?

• As people got tired of swinging, were they able to ask for help?

• Did the class show compassion for those who had a more difficult time swinging?

• Did the group value positive risk taking? Were there any examples of negative risk taking?

💡 Tips and Comments

• *Vary the boundaries depending on the ability of the group.*

• *If you have a student (or students) who cannot swing, introduce a role during the framing that allows one or two people to travel to the island "by air," etc., so that they can still spot but do not have to swing. (These students can simply walk, go by wheelchair or use whatever means is appropriate.)*

ASSESSMENT OPTION

Your class has been building a community since the start of the unit. How well are they doing? Use the Community Rubric (provided in the Assessment section near the end of this book) to help you assess the group's competency in this area.

Final Lesson: Putting It All Together, Grade 6

This final lesson wraps up the Adventure unit for Grade 6. The lesson is designed to provide students with time to celebrate the goals they have achieved, the chance to reflect on lessons learned, and an opportunity to consider how to transfer this learning to the rest of the year and to their lives.

Activities

We suggest that you choose activities from the whole range of activities that have already been done in this unit. Allowing class input as to what they would like to repeat for this final class can also be effective.

It is best to choose a variety of activities—some fun warmups, a couple of games that students have really enjoyed, and initiatives and low elements that they have done especially well, as well as one or two that may have been challenging for them. The number of activities selected depends on the length of the lesson you are hoping to lead. This lesson can easily take more than one class period.

Lesson Objectives

Students will be able to:

- Demonstrate respectful behaviors toward self, peers and adults
- Apply effective problem-solving strategies to accomplish group tasks
- Rely on the group to support appropriate risk taking
- Appropriately apply strengths and recognize weaknesses

Materials

- Dependent upon the activities selected
- Prewritten rules for each initiative that is going to be used

ACTIVITIES

Instructor's Choice (*see above*)

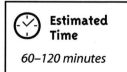

Estimated Time

60–120 minutes

Setup:
This lesson should be set up as a series of activities to be accomplished by the class. Arrange a series of initiatives and/or low elements in different locations that you can monitor. After some large group warmups and games, you may have to divide the class into smaller groups for the initiatives.

Framing:

Say to students, "As a way to end our Adventure unit, we are going to have a second chance to do some of our favorite games and to complete some of our favorite and most challenging initiatives. The goal of this lesson is for the entire class to gain the largest number of points possible. Each small group is gaining points for the whole class. Remember to apply all that you have learned. "

Procedure:

1. Do some favorite warmups and large-group games.

2. Split the class into groups. Start each group at a different initiative.

3. Hand out rule sheets for each activity, and remind each group of important safety considerations. Give rule clarification as needed.

4. Give each group a specific amount of time in which to complete each initiative.

5. Create a scoring system that gives the most points for full completion, fewer points for partial completion, and perhaps even some points for exhibiting positive behaviors.

6. Each group needs to self-score and self-monitor rule infractions.

7. After the time limit is up, the groups should rotate until each group has had a chance to do each initiative.

8. Remind the class that they are all working toward the same ultimate goal.

9. If students ask if they can help other groups, let them — this means that they are learning how to collaborate!

Discussion:

Ask students:

• Did we as a class demonstrate in this lesson all that we have learned in our unit? What are the important things that we have learned?

• What key things have we learned that we can keep using during the rest of the school year?

• What are some key things we have learned that we can apply to our out-of-school lives?

Tips and Comments

- Try to select initiatives that take about the same amount of time to complete.

- Avoid initiatives that have one solution.

- You may want to select an initiative that students have done in a different year.

- If the initiative portion of this lesson takes more than one class, take notes as to where each group is at the end of class so that they can resume from similar starting points when they meet again.

Adventure Curriculum for
Physical Education

Grade 7

SCOPE AND SEQUENCE

SECTION 1: CREATING COMMUNITY

Lesson 1   Learning group members' names, developing effective relationships
Activities: Name by Name
                   Captain's Calling

Lesson 2   Promoting community and understanding within the group
Activities: Giants, Wizards and Elves
                   Bumpity Bump Bump Bump
                   Twizzle
                   Evolution
                   Whampum

SECTION 2: ESTABLISHING FULL VALUE NORMS

Lesson 1   Reviewing the concept and importance of a Full Value Contract
Activity: Full Value Speed Rabbit

Lesson 2   Creating a Full Value Contract for the group
Activities: Dolphin Golf
                   Circle of Hands

Lesson 3   Putting the group's Full Value Contract into practice
Activity: Stargate

SECTION 3: PROBLEM SOLVING

Lesson 1 Beginning problem solving, reviewing of the ABCDS's of Problem
Activities: Pigs in a Blanket
Twirlie Bull's-Eye

Lesson 2 Setting achievable goals while problem solving
Activity: Mass Pass

Lesson 3 Finding, improving and refining solutions to problems
Activity: Key Punch

SECTION 4: BUILDING TRUST

Lesson 1 Recognizing and incorporating physical and emotional support in the group
Activities: Raccoon Circles
Hog Call

Lesson 2 Monitoring the safety of others in the group
Activities: Moving Without Touching
Ready Aim

Lesson 3 Exploring trust, reinforcing Challenge by Choice
Activity: I Trust You But. . .

SECTION 5: EXPERIENCES USING LOW ELEMENTS

Lesson 1 Respecting strengths and weaknesses, supporting positive
Activity: Whale Watch

Lesson 2 Participating fully, using group coordination to accomplish a task
Activity: Do I Go?

Lesson 3 Higher level problem solving
Activity: Islands

Final Lesson: Putting It All Together
Activities: Determined by facilitator

Section 1: Creating Community

LESSON 1

This is an introductory lesson. The primary focus of the lesson is for students to learn each other's names and to begin developing effective classmate relationships.

Activities
- Name by Name
- Captain's Calling

Lesson Objectives
Students will be able to:
- Recognize each person in the class by name
- Work together as a new group
- Experience and participate in the community
- Demonstrate positive working relationships with each other

Materials
- Boundary markers

ACTIVITIES

Name by Name

Estimated Time

15 minutes

Setup:
Gather the new class in a circle.

Framing:
Explain that they are going to do a naming activity together.

Procedure:
1. Ask each person in the circle to say his or her first name loudly and clearly. For fun, you can add that anyone who can't hear a name is allowed to yell, as loudly as possible, "Repeat." Demonstrate this to give students a laugh and to help break the new group tension that most likely exists. Depending on how hard you would like to make this task, you may have students repeat their names.
2. Explain that no one is allowed to speak, draw or show any identification. The class must now get into a circle as quickly as possible, arranging themselves in alphabetical order by their first names. Give them a starting place for *A*'s.

3. Once the group is settled and people agree that they are in the correct formation, have students say their names again. Allow the class to make silent adjustments until they have succeeded in arranging themselves in perfect order.

Discussion:

Ask students:

- Did you think this would be possible to do in only one or two attempts?
- What strategies did you use to get into place quickly?
- Let's remember what made us successful as we move into the next activity!

✓ **Safety Check**

This is a low-impact activity.

💡 **Tips and Comments**

• *This activity can be harder or easier depending on how much information you allow students to have at the start. We have seen large groups get into position quickly after hearing names only once, even though they have learned what the actual task is after hearing the names. Don't make it too easy!*

Captain's Calling

Setup:

Gather the class into a circle so that you can brief them on the following activity.

Framing:

Say to students, "There are many things that happen on a ship, from waltzing to cleaning the deck! This game involves acting out different situations very quickly."

Procedure:

1. Teach your group the following motions, and encourage them to make up some of their own too. These will serve as the commands of the ship:

- (1 person) "Attention"—Students stand at attention until the person who is designated Captain says, "At ease."
- (1 person) "Swab the Deck"—Make a mopping motion.
- (2 people) "Captain's Waltz"—Do a waltz-type-move with a partner.
- (3 people) "Lifeboats Out"—Form a single-file line, sit down and pretend to row a boat really quickly.
- (4 people) "Captain's Table"—Stand in a square and eat, very politely of course.

⏱ **Estimated Time**

30 minutes

✓ **Safety Check**

*Clear the play area
of any obstacles.*

- (5 people) "Starfish"—Put both hands in the center of the fivesome and spin around.
- (Everybody) "Person Overboard"—Everyone who has had to go out can now come back into the game by being "rescued" by other passengers.

2. Point out the boundaries of the ship to your students. Half of a basketball court-size works well.

3. Determine where the *bow* (front), *stern* (back), *port* (left) and *starboard* (right) are in relation to the boundaries. These will become commands, too. *Overboard* is directly outside *port* and *starboard*.

4. Explain to your class that when they hear one of the above commands, they are to follow the directions as quickly as possible. Anyone who is not able to follow the commands must go "overboard" until "Person Overboard" is called. For example, if "Lifeboats Out" is called, and a student is not able to find a place in a three-person lifeboat, that student will go overboard.

5. If the Captain calls "Attention" and does not say "At ease," students should not move. If they do, send 'em overboard!

6. If the Captain calls, "Bow," "Stern," "Port" or "Starboard," students are to run to that side of the ship as quickly as possible.

Discussion:
None necessary.

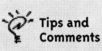 **Tips and Comments**

- *Offer students the chance to be the Captain. In this role, they can also make up new commands.*
- *You may skip the option of calling out "Bow," "Stern," "Port" and "Starboard."*
- *You may want to start the activity by demonstrating only a few motions. Then, once your students have a sense of how the activity works, you can add more commands and motions.*

ASSESSMENT OPTION

In the Assessment section near the back of this book, you will find an assessment tool called the Respect for Differences Project. This can be an ongoing assignment used throughout this unit that can be incorporated into the final evaluation.

In this lesson, students will play together and enjoy a series of activities that continue to promote a sense of community and understanding among group members.

Activities

- Giants, Wizards and Elves;
- Bumpity Bump Bump Bump
- Twizzle
- Evolution
- Whampum

Lesson Objectives
Students will be able to:

- Recognize each person in the class by name
- Work together as a new group
- Experience and participate in the community
- Understand that the differences students bring to class are valuable

Materials

- 15–20'-long rope
- 4 cones or suitable markers
- Boffer or "sword" made from newspaper or rigid foam

ACTIVITIES

Giants, Wizards and Elves

Setup:
Place the rope in the middle of a room or large open area. This will act as a dividing line. Place 2 cones approximately 20 yards from the rope on one side, and two cones 20 yards from the rope on the other side.

Framing:
The rules of play (described below) will serve as the frame for this game.

Procedure:

1. Divide the class in half; place each group on opposite sides of the rope. Have students stand with their toes on the line, then take two steps backward.

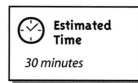
Estimated
Time
30 minutes

✓ Safety Check

- *Encourage appropriate tagging.*

- *Emphasize that the areas behind the cones are "safe zones."*

- *If playing outside on wet grass or a bumpy field, be sure to point these conditions out to the group and emphasize that safety is needed when running.*

2. Demonstrate the three signs that students will need to know:

   - "A Giant stands up on tiptoes, keeps arms raised overhead, and gives loud roars." Demonstrate, and have students practice.

   - "A Wizard stands on one foot, puts her hands in front of her, wiggles her fingers, and says 'Shazaam!' " Demonstrate, and have students practice.

   - "An Elf squats down, puts his hands behind his head, and yells 'Tweedle, tweedle, tweedle.' Of course, he uses a squeaky elfish voice." Demonstrate, and have students practice. Make sure that students know all three signs.

3. Explain that Giants chase Wizards, Wizards chase Elves and Elves chase Giants. Be sure that the class understands this progression. The goal of the activity is for each group to win members from the other group until there is only one group left! Here is how...

4. Each group huddles together behind their cones and selects a sign that they will make to represent their group (either a Giant, a Wizard or an Elf). All members of each team agree to make the same sign. Give them 45 seconds to do this; have them also pick a backup sign in case the other group picks the same one!

5. Have the students return to two steps behind their ropes. On the count of three, the groups simultaneously give their signs. The group that becomes the chasers (based on their sign and the other group's sign) tries to tag flee-ers before they run behind their cones. When tagged, flee-ers join the chasing group. For example, group A shows Wizards as their sign, group B shows Elves. Group A becomes the chasers and group B the flee-ers. Any of the group B students who are tagged must then join the A team.

6. After each round, groups should reassemble behind their cones to each pick another sign. The game continues until there is only one group left.

Discussion:

Ask students:

- What did you do as a group to make this game fun?

- How did your group decide which sign to make? How did you come to agreement?

- Is there anything that you would do differently?

💡 Tips and Comments

- *It can be hard to remember who chases whom, so do a few warmup rounds. Remind students that this is like a large Rock-Paper-Scissors game.*

- *You can use designations other than Giants, Wizards and Elves. Have the class make up their own.*

Bumpity Bump Bump Bump

Estimated Time

20 minutes

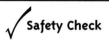

Safety Check

No special safety procedures required for this activity.

Setup:
Gather the class in a small circle, with you standing in the middle.

Framing:
Say to students, "In this game, you will start by knowing just your neighbors. By the end, you will know everyone in the 'neighborhood.' "

Procedure:

1. Have the class practice saying "Bumpity bump bump bump" as quickly as they can.

2. Explain that you will be pointing to someone in the circle and saying either "Left" or "Right," immediately followed by "Bumpity bump bump bump." The person that you point to must respond by saying the correct name of his or her neighbor on the side that you have designated before you finish saying "Bumpity bump bump bump." If this isn't done, that player must then go to the middle.

3. In addition to "Left" and "Right," you can add "You" and "Me." These would require players to say either their own name or your name. You can also come up with other creative variations.

Discussion:
Ask students:

- Does everyone know each other's names?

- Can some people learn names more easily than others? How about being in the middle—was that easier for some than for others? Are differences valuable?

Tips and Comments

- As players begin to learn each other's names, reduce the "Bumpity bump bump bump" to "Bumpity bump bump " or even "Bumpity bump." You can also add more variations, such as "Skip right." or Skip left."

- Add a second or third person in the middle to keep the action going quickly, particularly in larger groups.

- Add "Bow To": If a student is stuck in the middle for a long time and seems to be getting frustrated, suggest that he or she bow to another classmate, who will then take this player's place in the middle.

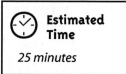

Estimated Time

25 minutes

✓ **Safety Check**

• *This activity should be played on level ground.*

• *Don't call "Twizzle" more than three times in a row.*

Twizzle

Setup:
Have students form a large circle around you.

Framing:
No special framing necessary.

Procedure:

1. Explain that this is a Simon Says type of game. There are five commands that students need to learn. The commands are:
   - Go—Walk in the direction that you are facing.
   - Stop—Stop moving and freeze.
   - Turn—Make a half-turn (180°) and freeze, keeping both feet on the ground.
   - Jump—Jump and make a half-turn, then freeze.
   - Twizzle—Jump and make a full turn (360°), then freeze.

2. Explain that the name of the game is Twizzle and that you will all be warming up to play a serious round of Competition Twizzle. Have students practice following the commands while you call them out. Players do need to be reminded to "freeze" after each command (except, of course, "Go").

3. After a few practice minutes, play a round with no one being eliminated. Do this until you think everyone knows the commands.

4. Announce that the class is now ready for Competition Twizzle, after they have each taken a very important oath. Say, "Students, raise your right hand and repeat after me: *In this game of Competition Twizzle, I understand that the referee is right. I will not argue with the referee, and so it is said and so it is done.*" After taking the oath, students will not be allowed to argue.

5. Begin the competition! When students are eliminated by not doing the correct command, they join you in the middle and become additional referees. Any grumbling from the competitors elicits a quick reminder of the oath that they have taken. The round ends when there are just three or four people left. Play a few rounds, since players usually want a second chance.

Discussion:
Usually none needed, unless following directions proves to be difficult.

 **Tips and Comments**

Keep the pace moving. Too slow a Twizzle game becomes a boring one!

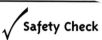
Evolution

Setup:
Gather your group in a circle to hear the briefing for this activity

Framing:
Say to students, "Remember the game Rock, Paper, Scissors?" (Review the game if necessary.) "In this game, that will be how we help each other evolve from being little Eggs to being Supreme Beings!"

Procedure:
1. The characters in the game are:

    Egg—Students crouch down and can waddle around.

    Chicken—Students put their hands under their armpits, flap their "wings" and make chicken sounds.

    Dinosaur—Students put their hands above their heads and make roaring sounds.

    Supreme Being—The group can make up their own motion and character, or see Tips and Comments on the following page.

2. The objective of the game is to have everyone end up as a Supreme Being.

3. Everyone starts out as an Egg. Eggs will waddle around to other Eggs and engage in a round of Rock, Paper, Scissors.

4. Whoever wins that round of play gets to evolve to the next character. For example, the winning Egg would become a Chicken.

5. Chickens then look for other Chickens with whom to play Rock, Paper, Scissors, and so on.

6. The person who loses the round of Rock, Paper, Scissors must de-evolve to the next lowest character. An Egg who loses the round will stay an Egg.

7. Only like characters can play Rock, Paper, Scissors with like characters. For example, a Chicken cannot challenge an Egg to a round of play. One exception is described below.

8. Once students have reached the Supreme Being status, they may approach any character at any level and play a round of Rock, Paper, Scissors. Because they are Supreme Beings, they cannot be stripped of this status, so there is no de-evolving if they lose. But, if the lesser character wins, that character gets to evolve.

9. Supreme Beings will need to look out for those less evolved to help get the whole class to the Supreme Being status.

10. Once everyone has fully evolved, the activity is over.

> **✓ Safety Check**
>
> *Students with knee problems will be uncomfortable crouching like Eggs. Permit them to stand in an alternative position.*

Discussion:

Ask students:

- What helped the entire class get to the Supreme Being status?
- What was the outcome of helping others to evolve?
- What can we learn about helping each other from this activity?

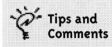

Tips and Comments

- *The Supreme Being motion can be something light and fun. Choosing Diana Ross (of The Supremes) as the Supreme Being will get a giggle; the motion can be singing a verse of "Stop in the Name of Love." The game can end with the song being sung by the entire class.*

- *This game can get some giggles from your students, so trust that once you start playing, they will get into it. Vary the level of silliness according the readiness of your class.*

- *Play another round with characters that have been thought up by students.*

Estimated Time

20 minutes

Whampum

Setup:

Have students sit in a circle with their legs extended out in front.

Framing:

Say to the group, "This is a more than a name game, it's a name plus game!"

Procedure:

1. Have each person give his or her name and say one thing that is personally important (for example, "Amy, and my dog, Willow").

2. After everyone in the circle has spoken, stand in the middle of the circle. Have someone start by saying another player's name and what is important to that person. You, as the middle person, try to "whack" the named person on the foot before he or she can name another person.

3. When you finally whack someone before that player says another's name and important thing, he or she must take your place in the circle.

4. If anyone flinches without due cause, that player then must move to the center position.

Discussion:

Ask students:

- Did anyone learn something about a classmate? Were there any surprises?
- Were we able to play and still take care of each other?

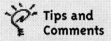

Tips and Comments

- *You can add a rule that the person leaving the middle of the circle needs to say the next name and important thing before sitting down, or that player can be tagged again! This keeps the game moving.*

- *You can also divide a larger group into smaller circles of 8 to 10 students after you have explained the game to the whole group.*

√ **Safety Check**

- *Boffers must be used only to hit feet.*

- *If students can't hit properly, the game should be stopped.*

- *Hits on the feet should be reasonably soft, as in a tag game. (You know that you're being tagged, but it doesn't hurt.)*

Section 2: Establishing Full Value Norms

LESSON 1

This lesson reviews the Full Value Contract from Grade 6 using a fun and engaging activity. Full Value Speed Rabbit is a game that involves everyone in a non-threatening way. We have found this to be a great de-inhibitizer that fits at almost any point in a program. Review of the core concept Challenge by Choice should also be incorporated here. This can be done with a simple discussion of Challenge by Choice, or you may choose to redo the Challenge Circle activity as it is described in Grade 6, Section 4, Lesson 1.

Activity
- Full Value Speed Rabbit

Lesson Objectives
Students will be able to:
- Understand the importance of creating a Full Value Contract for their class
- Recognize the five components of the Full Value Contract:

    Be Here
    Be Safe
    Be Honest
    Let Go and Move On
    Set Goals
- Understand and recognize behaviors that are consistent with the FVC
- Understand the concept of Challenge by Choice

Materials
- None needed for Full Value Speed Rabbit
- Rope for Challenge Circles if doing this activity

ACTIVITY

Full Value Speed Rabbit

Estimated Time

30 minutes

Setup:
Ask the class to stand in a circle, shoulder to shoulder. Have fun with the demonstration of this activity, and fully participate with the students to role-model enjoyable, zany behavior. It sets a lighthearted tone and reinforces the message that it is OK to try new things.

Framing:
Review the Full Value Contract that was used in grade 6. Explain to the class, "We will be playing a game using each of the Full Value Contract components:

- Be Here
- Be Safe
- Be Honest
- Let Go and Move On
- Set Goals"

Safety Check

No special safety procedures required for this activity.

Procedure:

1. Have the class develop a "statue" or "symbol" that represents each of the five Full Value components. These "symbols" are composed of three people each. Have the class practice making the various symbols; see below for symbol ideas.

2. Choose one person (the leader) to be in the center of the circle. The leader turns around and around in the circle, then randomly points to someone in the circle and calls out a symbol or Full Value component. The leader counts to five or ten, depending on how difficult you want to make the game.

3. The player who is pointed to becomes the main body of the statue; the people who are on either side of this player are the two sides. They must try to arrange themselves into this symbol before the leader finishes counting to ten. If they don't, the part of the statue that is not in place takes the leader's spot in the middle of the circle. If they are done in time, the leader stays put.

4. As the class learns the different symbols, add animals and other creative statues to the game.

5. Symbol or statue ideas: Have the class make up their own after you give them a few examples, like the following:

    Be Here: Center person stands in a sumo wrestler stance, with hands on hips. Side people each grab one of the "wrestler's" arms and pull, showing that the center person is "here."

    Be Safe: Center person waves a baseball "safe" sign while each of the side people puts a leg in the middle as if sliding into base.

    Let Go and Move On: Center person turns his or her back while the side people pretend to be letting go of a rope that they have been pulling on.

    Elephant: Center person extends left arm down and holds nose with right hand to form a trunk. Side people form ears by facing the center person and making a C shape with their arms.

    Rabbit: Center person uses hands to make rabbit ears on his or her head. Side people each stand near the center person while making a fast kicking/stepping motion with their legs like a rabbit.

Discussion:

- Have the class split into small groups. Ask each group to discuss one of the Full Value components.

- Students in each group should answer the question, "How will we know when we are doing our Full Value component and when we are not doing it."

- Have each group report out to the whole class.

- As a class, discuss how students will maintain the contract. Who is responsible for monitoring it?

Tips and Comments

- *Keep the game fun!*
- *Help each small group get specific about how to behave using their component of the FVC.*
- *Add all sorts of variations to the characters, and don't forget to let the class create their own symbols.*

This lesson is designed to give students an opportunity to really make the Full Value Contract their own. There is less activity and more facilitated discussion in this lesson, so be sure to provide students with an active warmup.

7.2.2

LESSON 2

Activities
- Dolphin Golf
- Circle of Hands

Lesson Objectives
Students will be able to:
- Practice setting personal goals that are achievable and that can be assessed
- Understand and recognize behaviors that are consistent with the FVC
- Develop the class-specific FVC
- Develop techniques to maintain the FVC
- Practice respectful behaviors toward self, peers and adults

Materials
- 4 rubber deck rings per small group of 2–4 students
- Large flipchart paper and markers

ACTIVITIES

Dolphin Golf

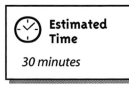

Estimated Time

30 minutes

Setup:
Break the class into groups of two to four players. Give each group about four deck rings. You may have set up a few golf holes already, using hazards, turns and obstacles to make them interesting. You can designate these using flags or cones.

Framing:
Say to students, "This activity will require you to set realistic goals and will give you a chance to achieve the goals that you set. Remember that Setting Goals is an important component of the FVC. You will have time now to practice catching and throwing the deck rings using the correct catching technique, which I will demonstrate." Teams should practice catching and throwing so that they have good information on which to base their goal setting.

Procedure:

1. Each small group, or team, will be playing a form of golf using the deck rings. The goal is for players to catch and throw the rings around the course in as few throwing attempts ("strokes") as possible.

2. A legal catch is one where the catcher extends one hand, fingers together and pointed upward, and the thrown ring lands to encircle the catcher's hand and arm. The catcher *may not* grab the ring with his or her fingers!

3. Students will quickly learn that the best throwing technique is to toss the deck rings in a Frisbee™-like fashion, so that they fly in a horizontal position. This makes catching them much easier.

4. When the round starts, each team decides what "par" each hole will be for them. The team's goal is to reach par. Teams track their own scores and the par of each hole.

5. Play starts with one team member running to a place along the hole where the ring can be caught successfully. The teammate who is throwing has four attempts to throw. The catcher is allowed to move from his or her spot only when the ring is in the air. When a successful catch is made, the next player on the team (or the thrower, if the team is a pair) moves to a new location. Each throwing attempt is one stroke.

6. If the thrower cannot hit the target after four attempts, a new thrower takes over.

7. At the end, have each team evaluate their score compared with their goal.

8. Play multiple rounds to improve scores.

Discussion:

This discussion is often best started in small groups, with groups then reporting out to the larger class. The whole class can also discuss these questions together.

• Did you successfully meet your goals? Why or why not?

• Were you able to set realistic goals on subsequent rounds? What made it easier to do that?

• What other Full Value behaviors were present during the activity? Let Go and Move On? Be Honest?

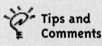 **Tips and Comments**

• *Try to make the course interesting. If you have the space, have students design their own holes.*

• *You can choose to set par for a course, or you can have students do so.*

• *Have the class come up with class goals in addition to small-group goals.*

Circle of Hands

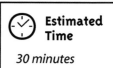

Setup:
The class should sit or stand around a large piece of flipchart paper that is positioned on the floor or on a tabletop. They should create a circle of hands by each tracing one of their hands onto the paper. Make a connecting line between each of these hands so that there is a clear inside and outside of the circle.

Framing:
Say to students, "We are using the five components of our Full Value Contract, but it is important that we really understand what they mean. Let's take some real examples from this class of how the contract has been working. We can use Dolphin Golf as our first example. Did people work well together? How? Were we honest? What did that look like?"

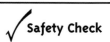

Safety Check

Safety here really centers around issues of emotional safety. Make sure that all voices are heard, and draw out ideas from the quieter members of the class.

Procedure:
1. As students begin stating behaviors or actions, write them down inside the circle of hands. You may need to lead students by asking questions and giving examples of actions that you have observed.

2. When the brainstorming has slowed down, remind the class, "We will return to this list for adjustment, but we will now focus on the things that can prevent us from using Full Value. What gets in the way of Letting Go and Moving On?" Write these ideas on the outside of the circle of hands.

Discussion:
Remind the class that components of the FVC will be revisited throughout the year. Ask them to keep these principles in mind and to use them as their guide for how to behave in this class.

Tips and Comments

• *Depending on the size of the class, you may want to do this first in small groups, then combine into a full-class circle of hands.*

• *Be open to students' ideas and suggestions…it is their contract, not just yours. At the same time, feel free to contribute, as you are also a member of the group.*

• *If the class uses catch phrases, like "We need to trust each other," ask them what this really means, or have them at least give examples of this quality in action.*

7.2.3

LESSON 3

In this lesson, focus on the FVC continues, but this time the class puts the contract into practice while completing an initiative. This will provide you with opportunities to test class behavior as it relates to the Full Value Contract that students have developed.

Activities
- Review Circle of Hands
- Stargate

Lesson Objectives
Students will be able to:
- Practice using the FVC to manage conflict within the group
- Practice respectful behaviors toward self, peers and adults

Materials
- The "circle of hands" (on paper) from the last lesson
- Hula Hoop™
- Markers

ACTIVITIES

Estimated Time

10 minutes

Review Circle of Hands

Ask students to review the circle of hands from the previous lesson. Ask if there is anything that they would like to add or remove.

Estimated Time

30 minutes

Stargate

Setup:
Have the class stand in a circle with joined hands. Ask two people in the circle to let go of each other and to hold onto the hoop with one hand.

Framing:
Say to students, "The goal of this activity is to get the entire class through the hoop as quickly as possible! This is a chance for us to not just talk about the Full Value

Contract, but to continue to practice it. Please be aware of the behaviors that we exhibit that are in the center of our circle of hands, and also be aware of any behaviors that are on the outside of that circle."

Procedure:

1. Each person must remain physically in contact with the rest of the class via at least one other person. The hoop holders must be in contact with both the class and the hoop.

2. If anyone else touches the hoop, the entire group starts again.

3. Cord holders can only hold the hoop with one hand each.

4. Ask the group to set a goal: How quickly do they think they can all get through the hoop?

5. Subsequent rounds can be played while making the time goal more challenging.

Discussion:

Ask students:

- In solving this problem, what things from the inside of our circle did we do?
- What things from the outside of the circle did we do?
- Did we do anything that we would like to add to the inside of our circle?
- Did we meet our goals? How and why?

After this discussion, it is important to ask the entire class to "buy into" the contract by signing their names to the circle of hands. This means that they agree to act in accordance to the contract at all times. This should then be saved or hung in an area where the class can refer to it and use it as an active FVC.

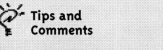
Tips and Comments

- *If you do not want to ask the class to hold hands, they can be given a long rope to hold instead.*
- *An elasticized cord also works well instead of the Hula Hoop.*
- *If using the cord, illustrate how it can snap back and sting people.*

ASSESSMENT OPTION

Especially if compassion is part of the group's Full Value Contract, utilize the Compassion—Peer Assessment tool provided in the Assessment section near the back of this book. Even if compassion is not explicitly stated in your class's contract, it is an integral component of any FVC. Remember also that peer assessments should not necessarily impact individual students' overall grades.

Safety Check

If participants move quickly during the activity, have them be aware of each other's shoulders and arms.

Section 3: Problem Solving

LESSON 1

This entertaining lesson offers a nice introduction to the problem-solving portion of the unit. There are many variations to each of these activities, so feel free to improvise and create your own initiative.

This is a good time to review the ABCDEs of Problem Solving, which students learned in Grade 6. This will give them a framework for doing the initiatives.

The ABCDEs of Problem Solving:

Ask questions to understand the problem.

Brainstorm solutions openly.

Choose a solution to implement.

Do it.

Evaluate that solution, adopt or discard it, and repeat this process if needed.

Activities

- Pigs in a Blanket
- Twirlie Bull's-Eye

Lesson Objectives

Students will be able to:

- Work together to achieve common goals
- Develop problem-solving techniques to accomplish group tasks
- Contribute their own and listen to others' ideas in the process of solving problems
- Follow procedures that are safe and effective for the given task

Materials

- Throwable items, including rubber pigs and/or chickens (have multiple items for each small group of about eight students)
- 1 tarp for each small group
- 1 twirlie for each student (have some extras on hand)
- 1–2 ropes to make a bull's-eye targets
- A larger boundary rope for the outside circle of the bull's-eye

ACTIVITIES

Pigs in a Blanket

Estimated Time

30 minutes

Safety Check

Use objects that are relatively light and soft.

Setup:
Ask the class to get into groups of about 8-10. Give each group a tarp to circle and to hold waist high.

Framing:
Say to students, "We are going to test how coordinated each group is! I will be giving you a series of instructions that each group must execute."

Procedure:

1. ***All catches and throws are done using the tarps.*** Start each group with their own rubber pig or chicken. Have groups practice throwing and catching their own item, using the tarp. Everyone must keep one hand on the tarp at all times.

2. Have each group demonstrate their highest toss.

3. Have each group demonstrate the highest number of consecutive tosses they can make.

4. Give each group another object of a different size and weight; have them repeat the above steps with that object.

5. Given their results, ask the class to select the item that they would like to use for the next series of tasks.

6. Each group is challenged to toss their object to another group, as well as to receive an object from that other group. You can keep score of how many successful throws and catches each group makes if that seems appropriate.

7. Do other variations if the group is still engaged.

Discussion:
Ask students:

- Was your group able to catch and throw the different objects successfully?
- What contributed to your success?
- Did everyone contribute to the solution? In what different ways did people contribute?
- Were you able to work effectively with another group? How?

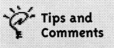

Tips and Comments

- *Have a variety of items available.*
- *Allow the students to make up their own variations.*

Estimated Time

30 minutes

Twirlie Bull's-Eye

Setup:
Explain this task before handing out the twirlies, or you will have lost the class for quite some time while they frivolously twirl away! Or, give each student a twirlie right away and allow for some unstructured fun. Warn students about potential eye injuries, and ask them to not twirl into the face of any classmate. For the Bull's-eye activity you will also need one or two targets (depending on the size of the class) and a large boundary circle around the target(s). Experiment with the size of the outside boundary.

Framing:
Explain that the class will be given a series of special practice activities, which will lead up to a final all-class goal.

Procedure:

1. Say to students, "The next few activities are warmups for a final goal-setting activity that you will be given. First, try and play 'twirlie catch' with a partner. See how many double catches the two of you can make—where you each catch your partner's twirly at the same time!" (This is a great opportunity for students to coach each other. Suggest this if it is not naturally occurring.)

2. Now say, "In foursomes, play a creative round of 'twirlie golf.' Pick targets that you all agree on, and count the number of strokes it takes you to reach the target."

3. When these warmups have been completed successfully, lead students into the final goal-setting activity. Ask them to stand around the boundary line. The class must agree upon the number of twirlies that they will successfully land in the bull's-eye. Emphasize that they have data to draw from – they know how they did during the practice rounds! The class should set their first goal prior to starting the activity.

4. Subsequent rounds should be held in order for the class to have opportunities to adjust their goal and to continue to improve their results.

Discussion:
Ask students:

- Did the class reach its goal?
- Was the goal realistic? Too hard? Too easy?
- How did you set the goal? What information did you use?
- What behaviors do you want the class to keep for the next goal-setting activity? What behaviors do you want to avoid?

💡 Tips and Comments

• *If the activity fails, the target may be too small. This activity is harder to do than it looks.*

• *As with Pigs in a Blanket, there are many variations still to be designed by educators like you. Have fun, and be creative.*

This lesson follows up on the goal-setting theme of the previous Twirlie Bull's-eye activity. The class is now given a different activity that requires everyone's participation and guides them to set achievable goals.

LESSON 2

Activity
- Mass Pass

Lesson Objectives
Students will be able to:
- Identify and practice using the different strengths of individuals in the group
- Work together to achieve common goals
- Develop problem-solving techniques to accomplish group tasks
- Contribute their own and listen to others' ideas in the process of solving problems
- Evaluate the effectiveness of their problem-solving process

Materials
- 1 Mass Pass Kit, obtainable from Project Adventure

ACTIVITY

Mass Pass

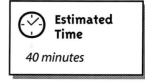
Estimated Time
40 minutes

Setup:
Using rope, create a fairly large square (15'–25' per side). Make sure that the square has clearly defined corners. In one corner of the square place one bucket (bucket #1), and in the opposite corner place the other bucket (bucket #2). Place all of the fleece balls and flying discs/deck rings into bucket #1.

Framing:
Tell students that this activity requires them to transport multiple objects around the perimeter of the square. Say, "The ability to plan effectively is needed to succeed, yet there is also opportunity for creative thinking in devising a strategy. I'll give you all the rules, and then I'll give you some time to plan."

Procedure:
1. The goal for the group is to increase their score over several (minimum of six) successive rounds, and to maximize their score in the last round. Give the following rules, and then allow for some planning time. Points are scored according to how many objects end up in bucket #2 over a 90-second period (round).

2. All objects must start inside bucket #1 at the beginning of every round.

3. Time for each round starts when the first object is removed from bucket #1.

4. All sides of the square must be occupied by at least one student.

5. Once a person has chosen a side of the square to stand on, she or he may not switch sides within a round.

6. Every participant must touch each object after it leaves bucket #1 and before it ends up in bucket #2.

7. Objects may not be passed to anyone to the immediate right or left; in other words, the object must "skip" at least one person when it is passed.

8. Points are earned for each object that is placed successfully inside bucket #2.

9. Whenever an object is being passed, it must always cross over the inside of the boundary area (i.e., it cannot be passed around the corner outside the perimeter of the square or behind anyone).

10. Whenever an object is dropped outside the boundary marker, it must be returned to the "resource container" (bucket #1) to be recycled, if it is to be used in the round.

11. If an object is dropped inside the boundary markers, it may not be retrieved and is lost for the duration of that round.

12. No member of the team may step inside the perimeter boundary during a round. If this occurs, all of the objects must be returned to the starting bucket.

13. All actions must stop when the time is up. At that time, students should count the objects in bucket # 2 and tally their score.

14. Scoring: 10 points for every fleece ball, 20 points for every disc or deck ring.

15. Give planning opportunities between each round so that the class can continually improve their time.

Discussion:

- Idea generation, time management, creative problem solving, listening, and inclusion are just some of the skills/issues that can emerge with this activity.

- Look for themes that emerge, and highlight one or two in your reflection time.

- Because this activity has multiple rounds, the discussion and problem solving in between rounds may be very rich. Therefore, a post-activity discussion could simply be a summary of those earlier discussions.

Tips and Comments

- *Because there are so many steps in preparing for this game, it may help your group if rules are either written on flipchart paper or handed out to students.*

- *To increase the challenge level of this activity, include different objects that have different point values—for example, include a rubber chicken that is worth 50 points.*

- *If you have a large group, increase the 90-second round time to 3 minutes.*

Problem-solving situations often involve finding solutions and then continuously improving and refining those solutions. This activity gives your class a chance to do just that.

7.3.3

LESSON 3

> **Activity**
> - Key Punch
>
> **Lesson Objectives**
> Students will be able to:
> - Identify and practice using the different strengths of individuals in the group
> - Work together to achieve common goals
> - Practice both leadership and followership in accomplishing group tasks
> - Develop problem-solving techniques to accomplish group tasks
> - Contribute their own and listen to others' ideas in the process of solving problems
> - Evaluate the effectiveness of their problem-solving process
> - Follow procedures that are safe and effective for the given task
> - Develop positive mechanisms to deal with failure
>
> **Materials**
> - Project Adventure Key Punch Set, obtainable through Project Adventure

ACTIVITY

Key Punch

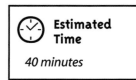

Estimated Time

40 minutes

Setup:

Make a rectangle with the boundary rope that is provided in the set. The rope should be about 80' long. Inside the rectangle, place 30 numbered spot markers in random order. Place the spots well inside the boundary so that they cannot be easily reached from outside the boundary. About 20–30 feet away, place a starting line.

Ask the class to stand behind the starting line. If you have a class of more than 15, use 2 groups. If the class numbers more than 30, you may want to consider 3 groups. Have different starting lines for each group; each group should be on a different side of the giant "keypad."

Framing:

Say to students, "You have been asked here today because you are experts on debugging large computers. The computer that you are challenged to fix is set here on the ground. What I *do* know is that the best way to fix this computer is to touch each number in sequence, from lowest to highest. The faster the numbers are touched, the greater the number of bugs that are removed from the program. You will be timed."

Procedure:

1. Only one player is allowed in the keypad area at one time.

2. Numbers must be touched in sequence.

3. Everyone in the class must touch at least one number.

4. The time starts when the first person crosses the starting line. Time stops when the last person crosses back over the starting (finish) line.

5. Ropes and spots may not be moved.

6. Although players may talk while at the pad, no planning can occur there, only execution of a plan.

7. Players have 30 minutes or 5 trials, whichever comes first, to achieve the fastest time possible.

8. The penalty for each rule infraction is 10 seconds added to that group's time for that particular trial. If a group has more than 1 person in the pad 5 different times during a trial, add 50 seconds to the total time of that trial.

If doing this with multiple groups, you can have all the groups sharing the same pad. However, only one group can be on the pad at one time. Unless you add to the story that all players are working for the same computer debugging company, (and even if you do...), there will be lots of competition between groups. This adds to the discussion at the end.

Discussion:

If multiple groups are involved, the discussion may work best in those separate groups. Ask students:

• Did your times decrease, resulting in continuous improvement?

• What contributed to this success (or lack of success)?

• Has the class improved in its problem-solving ability? Can we continue to improve?

• There were a lot of rules to follow. Were you able to do this? Did it get easier later in the activity?

• What did you do when mistakes were made?

• How were people's different strengths used?

• How were decisions made about what to do for each trial?

• [In cases of multiple groups] How did you work with the other groups using the pad? Did you share ideas or compete with them? Why?

Tips and Comments

• *Leaving out a keypad number or two adds a twist to the activity.*

• *You may also opt to have multiple pads for multiple groups to use separately.*

• *If there is only one teacher, ask one student in each group to be the timer and the penalty observer.*

• *If the group is ready for this, have them keep track of penalties themselves.*

ASSESSMENT OPTION

The Problem Solving—Group Assessment Checklist is an excellent way to assess the class's problem-solving ability. See the Assessment section near the end of this book.

Section 4: Building Trust

LESSON 1

In this lesson, students will do two activities that will require them to offer both physical and emotional support to those around them.

Activities
- Raccoon Circles
- Hog Call

Lesson Objectives
Students will be able to:
- Demonstrate reliable behaviors that offer physical and emotional support to others

Materials
- Rope circles—1 for every pair of students
- Blindfolds—1 per player (optional)

ACTIVITIES

Raccoon Circles

⏱ **Estimated Time**

20 minutes

Setup:
Have students select partners, or use a creative way to get them into pairs (e.g., "fold" a line of students in half; everyone partners with the facing person).

Framing:
Say to students, "We're all familiar with the expression 'Lean on me,' right? We're going to practice leaning on each other and giving each other support."

Procedure:
1. Explain the guidelines of the game before you give out the rope circles.
2. Explain that each circle of rope is there to help partners lean on each other.
3. Partners should stand facing each other with the rope in their hands. They should then practice leaning back, trying to trust each other and the rope.
4. Proper position includes students standing with their feet about shoulder width apart and bodies in a stiff position.

5. Instruct students that if they feel as if they are going to fall over, they should step forward or backward.

6. After partners have leaned fully out from the rope, they may then sit down while maintaining their lean, then attempt to stand back up, without taking their hands off the rope.

Discussion:

Ask students:

- Were you and your partner able to lean with each other?
- What did physical support look like in this activity?
- What did emotional support look like in this activity?

Tips and Comments

For the rope circles, use rope or webbing tied in a loop with an appropriate knot (square knots with safeties work well with rope, and water knots work best with webbing).

Safety Check

Be sure that you are in a position to keep this activity controlled. Do not let pairs spread out too far, yet make sure that they are not so close together as to bump into each other when they are sitting and standing. Emphasize that students should be aware of when one partner is a different size than the other, so as to control who needs to lean more.

Hog Call

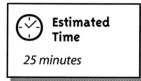
Estimated Time

25 minutes

Setup:

Have students keep the same partners from the previous activity.

Framing:

Say to the class, "We need to continue to support each other throughout our year in physical education. In this activity, you will all be blindfolded and will need to pay attention to safety and to each other in order to be successful. Remember, bumpers up."

Procedure:

1. Explain that you would like each partner group to select a pair of words that relate to the last activity. These words should represent something that has helped them, such as *Full-Value*, or *Physical-Support*, etc. Once each partner group has selected its words, have each individual within the pair select which of the two words will be his or hers.

2. Ask each pair to share their words with the class. Eliminate duplicates.

3. Designate two lines a good distance apart so that this activity is challenging. (Too small a space eliminates the discovery aspect of the activity.) Explain that each person from a partnership is to go behind a different line, in effect

splitting up each pair. Remind players to remember their words! They should be instructed to put on their blindfolds or close their eyes when they get behind their lines.

4. Once everyone is behind a line with eyes closed, ask players to move around to avoid having "prespotted" their partners across the way.

5. The object of the activity is for players to find their original word partners, keeping their eyes closed or their blindfolds on. Of course, this will involve lots of noise while players shout out their partner's words and try to listen for their own words being called out. (For example, if I were Full, I would yell Value, while my partner yelled Full, until we were finally standing next to each other. Pairs are only allowed to yell their own words, not others'.)

6. We have found it best to demonstrate what you mean by "shouting" a word. Give a loud bellow so that students feel free to make noise. Chaos adds to the fun and challenge of the activity.

7. Once pairs are together, have them remove their blindfolds. They should discuss a series of questions designated by you. The discussion should last 5 to 10 minutes. Questions can vary; examples might include questions about trust or team building.

8. If time permits, sit the class down. Have each pair quickly introduce each other and share a few of their partners' answers.

Discussion:

This activity may not require one. However, if you think it would benefit the group, ask students the following:

• How did you and your partner find each other?

• What was it like to be blindfolded?

• Did you learn anything about your partner in this activity?

• What behaviors from the FVC helped you support each other in this activity?

 **Tips and Comments**

• *Blindfolds can be very difficult for some students, so give them the option simply to close their eyes. In fact, in some settings it is not appropriate to introduce blindfolds at all.*

• *This activity can be fairly quick if you eliminate the discussion questions, or it can be quite lengthy if you have each pair introducing each other. For this curriculum, we suggest that you do encourage some discussion between partners.*

This lesson is designed to provide students with the opportunity to monitor the safety of their partners.

Activities
- Moving Without Touching
- Ready Aim

Lesson Objectives
Students will be able to:
- Demonstrate reliable behaviors that offer physical and emotional support to others
- Express their feelings in a supportive environment

Materials
- Blindfolds for half of the class (optional)
- Soft throwable objects—a minimum of one per person
- Boundary markers

ACTIVITIES

Moving Without Touching

Setup:
Outline an area with boundary markers that will be small enough so that the group won't get too spread out—about 25' 25' for 25 students. Have the group circle up while you give the instructions.

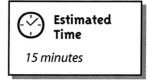

Estimated Time

15 minutes

Procedure:
1. Explain to the class that during this warmup activity, they will have a chance to practice moving like cars at different speeds.
2. Ask for some ideas about some things that help keep cars safe. Point out that car bumpers (as in "bumpers up," with students holding two hands up in front of their chest at all times), speed limits and avoiding collisions are extremely important.
3. Explain the different speeds, and challenge players to move at these speeds in the designated play area without any collisions (without touching any other student). Call each speed out loud, giving the class time to move appropriately.

Speeds are typically called out in ascending order, until the class has moved at the fastest speed. You can also vary the speeds once students have experienced each.

4. Some ideas for speeds are:

   Cars in jelly: Students move very, very slowly.

   Cars in water: Students still move very slowly, but slightly faster than at the jelly speed.

   Cars on a country road: Students use a normal walking pace.

   Cars in highway: Students use a fast walking/running pace.

5. After each round, check in to find out if players were indeed able to stay at the assigned paces before you move the group progressively faster.

Discussion:

Ask students:

- Were you able to keep all the cars safe? How?

- Were there any near misses? Why?

- How do we want to keep each other safe?

- What are the most important things to remember when we're moving around all at the same time?

- Is it OK to express feelings of frustration or feelings of elation in this class depending on how the activity is going? Does this help the group?

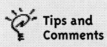 **Tips and Comments**

- *Once the class can use this language to regulate their speeds, they will be able to apply it to other moving activities. This will help you control pace.*

- *Have students come up with other symbols and motions.*

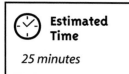 **Estimated Time**

25 minutes

Ready Aim

Setup:

Designate pairs. Have each pair select which one of them will be blindfolded first. These players should close their eyes or put on their blindfolds. Explain that the sighted partners cannot touch, retrieve or throw a ball.

Framing:

Say to students, "This activity requires that you pay close attention to safety. There will be one sighted and one blindfolded person in each pair. Sighted persons will be responsible for the safety of their partners."

Procedure:

1. The object of the game is for each blindfolded person to throw the ball and hit another blindfolded person. If a sighted person is hit, nothing happens, except that the sighted person can yell, "Missed me!" as obnoxiously as desired.

2. A sighted person may not physically touch the blindfolded partner. All communication is verbal. (Of course, if the blindfolded person is going to be injured, it is the sighted person's responsibility to help avoid that situation, regardless of whether it involves touching!)

3. As the teacher, you can throw balls back in bounds and add extra balls to the activity. After a period of time, partners should change roles.

Discussion:

Have players discuss these questions first with their partners. Then they can report out key ideas to the whole class.

- Were you more comfortable sighted or blindfolded? Why?
- How did you and your partner communicate? Was it effective?
- In what ways were you supported physically and emotionally?
- What would you do the same way the next time you are in an activity like this? What would you do differently?

Safety Check

- *Use appropriate soft balls.*
- *Assess the group's readiness to take care of each other before doing this activity.*
- *Bumpers up!*
- *Instruct players to exercise care when bending over to pick up balls so as not to bump heads with other players.*
- *Remember that emotional safety is critical to maintain when blindfolds are on.*

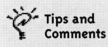

Tips and Comments

- *Make the playing area reasonably small so that there is enough action.*
- *You can choose to start each pair with two balls.*

ASSESSMENT OPTION

After this series of lessons, use the Compassion—Peer Assessment tool provided near the back of this book in the Assessment section. Compassion is an important component of trust, and receiving peer feedback can be invaluable. Remember that peer assessment does not have to be used as an evaluation tool that affects a student's overall grade. Use this tool wisely.

LESSON 3

This lesson begins to explore trust in the class. It can also reinforce Challenge by Choice in a setting where levels of trust may vary greatly.

Activity
- I Trust You But…

Lesson Objectives
Students will be able to:
- Understand the concept of Challenge by Choice in a risk-taking setting
- Understand that progressive personal challenges, within a safe environment, can lead to increased self-awareness and learning opportunities
- Learn the importance of respecting and supporting the different decisions of others regarding personal levels of challenge

Materials
- 1 blindfold (optional)

ACTIVITY

I Trust You But…

Estimated Time
40 minutes

Setup:
No special setup necessary.

Framing:
Say to students, "Often when you do something that is very hard, or even a bit scary or unknown, it is easier if you have your friends around to help you. In this activity, the class will be here to help you. Remember Challenge by Choice? In this activity, you can choose your own level of challenge by deciding to walk, jog or run. The rest of the class will be here to support your level of challenge and to spot you."

Procedure:
1. If you are doing this outside, have the first student walk across the field to a good distance away (75 yards or so). This person is now the runner. Ask the runner to take a look back at the group, then to shut his or her eyes or put on the blindfold. The rest of the class should position themselves in a cone-shaped

configuration at the runner's destination point. The runner is to run, blindfolded, toward the group. The group's job is not to let the runner stray too far and to stop the runner when he or she gets to the stopping/destination point. They do this by keeping Bumpers up and by gently guiding the runner in the correct direction.

2. Prior to starting, have the blindfolded runner yell to the class, "Ready to spot me?" The class should respond, "Ready." Spotters, after giving their response, should remain silent.

3. At this point the blindfolded person is to walk, jog or run at a steady pace toward the ending point. The trick is for the runner to keep this steady pace and to trust that the spotters will keep him or her from harm.

4. Place a few spotters along the route to prevent a wildly erratic runner from going astray.

Safety Check

• *Assess the readiness of the class to stay attentive and take this seriously.*

• *Make sure you have enough students to funnel the runner safely to the ending point.*

• *Only one runner at a time!*

Discussion:

Ask students:

- Was it hard or easy to trust your classmates to keep you safe?

- Did anyone feel safer blindfolded than as a spotter?

- How did it feel to be the only nonsighted person?

- How can we support each other in future activities when things get hard or scary? How about in places other than class?

- Did you feel that it was OK to not do this activity? To choose "no"? Did the class support this?

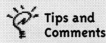

Tips and Comments

• *Indoors, have the runner start at one wall and run to another. The rest of the class should be lined up against the target wall, ready to intercept the runner.*

• *This activity is harder than it looks!*

Section 5: Experiences Using Low Elements

LESSON 1

This is the first outdoor low element of the unit. It also happens to be one of the most versatile low elements that you can have on your site. This lesson offers only one example of how the element can be introduced and approached. Students of all physical abilities will find this an engaging element.

Activity
- Whale Watch

Lesson Objectives
Students will be able to:
- Apply their own strengths and weaknesses appropriately
- Respect others' strengths and weaknesses
- Rely on the group to support positive risk taking

Materials
- 1 Whale Watch platform, obtainable through Project Adventure

ACTIVITY

Whale Watch

Estimated Time

40 minutes

Setup:
Check to make sure that the activity begins with the platform in a balanced position. Have the class help you reposition the platform if necessary.

Framing:
Say to students, "This platform represents your Full Value Contract. Can we call out some of the components of our contract? The contract always needs to stay in balance—which, as we have learned, takes some work. What are some things that we need to do to keep our contract balanced? What are some of the negative influences on our contract?

Your task today is to have everyone on the platform while keeping it in balance."

Procedure:

1. The entire class must get onto the platform. Players can only enter from one of the two ends.

2. Once the class is on and balanced, the task is for the group on each side to change places with the group on the opposite side. However, the platform should touch the ground on either side as few times as possible.

3. An optional additional task is to have everyone exit the platform, still keeping the platform in balance.

4. No one is allowed to stand in the middle; this area can only be stepped on in passing.

5. Students are not allowed to hold the platform if they are not on the platform.

6. Before they begin, the class must decide on how many times they will allow the platform to touch the ground on either side during this entire exercise.

7. Ask the class to be their own monitors as far as the number of times either end of the platform touches the ground.

Discussion:

With partners, students should discuss the following:

- Did the group manage the Full Value Contract well during this activity?

- Think about how you personally helped this activity succeed. What were some of the ways? Are these some of your strengths?

- What did you personally do to not help the group succeed? Is this an area where you can improve?

- Did the group support people taking risks?

- What different roles were needed during this exercise?

 **Safety Check**

- *Show the weight and movement of the platform before allowing students on.*

- *Feet can get pinched under the platform. Be sure to create a one-foot-wide zone around the platform perimeter so that feet and legs are not trapped or scraped as the platform moves.*

- *When asking the class to get on or off the platform to start or end the initiative, tip the platform to one end so that they can easily step on or off.*

- *Exits should be controlled so that no one is surprised.*

Tips and Comments

Some groups will elect to tip the platform to one side, have everyone get on, briefly balance the platform, tip it again and have everyone change places and exit. This certainly changes the difficulty of the activity. You may want to explain that that is not allowed during the briefing, or let them do it and congratulate them on a creative solution.

7.5.2

LESSON 2

This activity is more physically challenging than the Whale Watch and still requires the entire class to participate fully. This is less of a problem-solving experience than some other low-element activities, but it does require full group coordination.

Activity
- Do I Go?

Lesson Objectives
Students will be able to:
- Physically challenge themselves in a safe environment
- Apply their own strengths and weaknesses appropriately
- Respect others' strengths and weaknesses
- Rely on the group to support positive risk taking
- Identify how fatigue can lead to injury

Materials
- 1 Multiswing rope, obtainable through Project Adventure
- 4 All Aboard or Prouty's Landing platforms, obtainable through Project Adventure

. . . .

ACTIVITY

Do I Go?

Estimated Time

40 minutes

Setup:
Set up the Multiswing rope, being sure to leave a loop in the bottom of the rope. Position the platforms at four opposite sides around the swing rope (see diagram below). These platforms will be just inches off the ground.

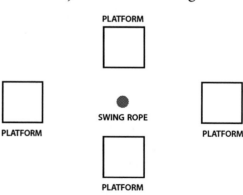

Framing:

Say to students, "You are being given a chance to travel around the world—to visit the East, the West, the South and the North. Everyone must go to each corner of the world and stand on the platform there for at least five seconds in order to have made a brief visit to that region of the world."

Start by placing an equal number of people at each "corner of the world."

Procedure:

1. Everyone must touch each platform and stay positioned on that platform for at least five seconds.
2. No one is allowed to touch the ground either around the platform or on the area between platforms.
3. No one is allowed into the swing area to retrieve the rope if it ends up hanging back in the "middle of the world."
4. To start, or in the event that the rope ends up back in the middle, the class is asked to figure out a way to retrieve the rope. Throwing objects at it to get it to swing, or hooking it with some object in the area or with a string of jackets or shoes, usually accomplishes this. Of course, you may give them the rope at the start if you prefer. This is a way to vary the difficulty and/or the timing of the activity.

Discussion:

Ask students:

- How was the plan communicated between the different parts of the world?
- Was each part of the world always informed about what was going on?
- What did, or did not, help communication?
- How were people helped? If some participants became fatigued, how did others assist them?
- During the activity, were you able to demonstrate some personal strengths? Share these with a partner.
- Did the group support the risk taking of individuals?

Safety Check

- *Make sure that students have practiced with a swing rope (a hang test) before doing this activity*
- *Have spotters nearby and watching as students step into the foot loop.*
- *The teacher may need to spot students as they swing.*
- *Instruct students to swing gently onto each platform. They must not kick their feet at people standing on the platform.*
- *If students feel that they are going to fall off a platform, they should step off so as not to take anyone else with them.*
- *If students are going to let go of the swing rope, they should first put one or two feet down to stop their swing.*

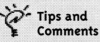

Tips and Comments

- *Make the distance between the swing rope and the platforms reasonable.*
- *You should test the swing yourself to make sure it is OK.*
- *Remember that sideways swings are harder than in-line swings.*

ASSESSMENT OPTION

How is the class progressing in terms of community development? Assess this through reading students' journal responses. Their insights are very telling. Use the Community Journal Questions provided in the Assessment section near the back of this book.

7.5.3

LESSON 3

This initiative will require a higher level of problem solving than Do I Go? It is less physically active, however, so you may want to plan active warmup and wrap-up activities for the class.

Activity
- Islands

Lesson Objectives
Students will be able to:
- Physically challenge themselves in a safe environment
- Respect their own strengths and weaknesses
- Respect others' strengths and weaknesses
- Rely on the group to support positive risk taking
- Demonstrate proper spotting techniques

Materials
- Installed Island platforms, about 8' apart, or 3 portable platforms set 8' apart (both obtainable through Project Adventure)
- 2 boards, 4' and 6' in length

ACTIVITY

Islands

⏱ **Estimated Time**

45 minutes

Setup:
Make sure that the boards do not reach between the "islands" by themselves. If the Islands are not fixed, be sure that they are properly positioned and secure. The platforms should be a foot or so off the ground.

Review spotting techniques from last year. Practice them with the class as necessary. (If low elements were not done the previous year, a spotting lesson may be required.)

Framing:
Say to students, "There is a major epidemic on its way. You will be stranded in this school for the rest of your life if you do not get to the final platform without touching the ground. For any of you ever to leave the school, all of you must get to that final platform." Be sure to explain all safety considerations.

Procedure:

1. The class starts either on or behind the first "island." Once they are standing on the island, they may not touch the ground again until they have traveled to the final platform.

2. If any participant touches the ground, the entire class must go back to the beginning.

3. If a board touches the ground, choose an appropriate penalty for the level of your class. Often this consists of sending one person of the class's choice back to the start. However, you may decide to send more back if you like.

Discussion:

Have students address the following:

- In pairs, discuss the various roles that were taken on during the activity and which roles each of you played.

- In pairs, list three examples of how risks were taken during the activity.

- In pairs, discuss what you have learned about solving problems during the low-element portion of this unit. Share your thoughts with the class.

Tips and Comments

- *Make sure that the starting platform can accommodate the entire class, with some room to spare.*

- *With a very large class, this initiative may be too cumbersome and slow.*

- *Using two sets of Islands is the best solution for large classes.*

ASSESSMENT OPTION

How are students feeling about themselves? Physical education and Adventure can positively impact self-esteem. Assess your students' self-esteem using the Self-Esteem Self-Assessment tool included in the Assessment section near the back of this book.

Safety Check

- *Follow spotting procedures as stated in the Project Adventure Safety Manual or as learned in your training.*

- *Make sure that the platforms are sturdy and that their supports are placed on solid ground.*

- *Illustrate proper lifting techniques so that students do not hurt their backs moving the boards.*

- *Remind students to be careful not to hit anyone with the boards as they move them.*

- *Watch that students do not get their fingers pinched under the boards.*

- *Watch that the boards do not slip to the left or right while people are on them.*

- *Spot as needed.*

7.F

FINAL LESSON

Final Lesson: Putting It All Together, Grade 7

This final lesson wraps up the Adventure unit for Grade 7. This lesson is designed to provide students with time to celebrate the goals they have achieved, the chance to reflect on lessons learned, and an opportunity to consider how to transfer this learning to the rest of the year and to their lives.

Activities

We suggest that you choose activities from those that have already been done in this unit. Allowing class input as to what they would like to repeat for this final class can also be effective.

We suggest that you choose a variety of activities: some fun warmups, a couple of games that students have really enjoyed, and initiatives and low elements that they have done especially well, as well as one or two that may have been challenging for them. The number of activities selected depends on the length of the lesson you are hoping to lead. This lesson can easily take more than one class period.

Lesson Objectives:

Students will be able to:

- Demonstrate respectful behaviors toward self, peers and adults
- Apply effective problem-solving strategies to accomplish group tasks
- Rely on the group to support appropriate risk taking
- Appropriately apply strengths and recognize weaknesses

Materials

- Dependent upon the activities selected
- Prewritten rules for each initiative that is going to be used

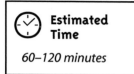

Estimated Time

60–120 minutes

ACTIVITIES

Instructor's Choice *(see above)*

Setup:

This lesson should be set up as a series of activities to be accomplished by the class. Have a series of initiatives and/or low elements set up in different locations that you can monitor. After some large-group warmups and games, you may have to divide the class into smaller groups for the initiatives.

Framing:

Say to students, "As a way to end our Adventure unit, we are going to have a second chance to do some of our favorite games and to complete some of our favorite and most challenging initiatives. The goal of this lesson is for the entire class to gain the largest number of points possible. Each smaller group is gaining points for the whole class. Remember to apply all that you have learned."

Procedure:

1. Do some favorite warmups and large-group games.

2. Split the class into groups. Start each group on a different initiative.

3. Hand out rule sheets for each activity, and remind each group of important safety considerations. Give rule clarification as needed.

4. Give each group a specific amount of time in which to complete each initiative.

5. Create a scoring system that gives the most points for full completion, fewer points for partial completion, and perhaps even some points for exhibiting positive behaviors.

6. Each group needs to self-score and self-monitor rule infractions.

7. After the time limit is up, groups should rotate until each group has had a chance to do each initiative.

8. Remind the class that they are all working toward the same ultimate goal.

9. If students ask if they can help other groups, let them—this means that they are learning how to collaborate!

Discussion:

Ask students:

- Did we as a class demonstrate in this lesson all that we have learned in our unit? What are the important things that we have learned?

- What key things have we learned that we can we keep using during the rest of the school year?

- What are some key things we have learned that we can apply to our out-of-school lives?

Safety Check

- *Be sure that the class is ready to work independently on the activities you select.*

NOTE: Be sure that you choose activities that can be self-managed by the students as there will be multiple groups working simultaneously. If your class cannot manage this, or you would like to choose activities that do require adult supervision, we recommend that you have additional teachers and/or parent volunteers serving as dependable spotters during this session.

- *Stop action, and subtract points, if safety procedures are not followed.*

- *Review all of the safety rules for each activity before starting.*

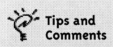
Tips and Comments

- *Try to select initiatives that take about the same amount of time to complete.*

- *Avoid initiatives that have one solution, such as Mergers.*

- *You may want to select an initiative that students have done in a different year.*

- *If the initiative portion of this lesson takes more than one class, take notes as to where each group is at the end of class so that they can resume from similar starting points when they meet again.*

Adventure Curriculum for
Physical Education

Grade 8

SCOPE AND SEQUENCE

SECTION 1: CREATING COMMUNITY

Lesson 1   Learning group members' names, sharing commonalities and differences
Activities: Categories
           Peek-a-Who

SECTION 2: ESTABLISHING FULL VALUE NORMS

Lesson 1   Problem solving as a lead-in to developing the group's Full Value Contract
Activities: Turnstile
           The Village

Lesson 2   Reviewing and putting the Full Value Contract into practice
Activities: Full Value Speed Rabbit
           Group Juggle

SECTION 3: PROBLEM SOLVING

Lesson 1   Performing initiatives requiring creative thinking in a changing environment
Activities: Change Up
           Overhand Knot

Lesson 2   Evaluating and refining problem solving skills, thinking "out of the box"
Activities: Mergers
           Pipeline

Lesson 3   Finding solutions, coordinating the group's problem solving efforts
Activity: The Meuse

SECTION 4: BUILDING TRUST

Lesson 1   Developing trust while increasing levels of personal commitment
Activities: Trust Leans
                Three-Person Leans
                Wind in the Willow
                Levitation

SECTION 5: EXPERIENCES USING LOW ELEMENTS

Lesson 1   Applying previous learnings to new tasks
Activity: Disc Jockeys

Lesson 2   Communicating, supporting, taking positive risks, respecting differences while solving a
                problem, applying proper spotting
Activity: Mohawk Walk

Lesson 3   Supporting others during individual challenges
Activity: Low Climbing Wall Traverse

Lesson 4   Fully participating in problem solving
Activity: Spider's Web: People Version

Final Lesson: Putting It All Together
Activities: Determined by facilitator

Section 1: Creating Community

LESSON 1

This lesson introduces students to each other and gives them an opportunity to learn each other's names as well as to share some commonalities and differences that exist among them.

Activities
- Categories
- Peek-a-Who

Lesson Objectives
Students will be able to:
- Create a sense of community
- Recognize each person in the group by name
- Understand that the differences people bring to class are valuable

Materials
- A tarp or sheet

. . . .

ACTIVITIES

Categories

Estimated Time

20 minutes

Setup:
None needed.

Framing:
Say to students, "We all have some things in common and many things that are different. This activity will give us a chance to discover some of these things."

Procedure:
1. Now say, "I am going to ask a series of questions. When you give each answer, you are to find other people who have given similar answers and stand together. If no one shares your answer, stand alone."
2. After answering each question (see Sample Questions under Tips and Comments below), students should find others who have common responses and stand together in groups.

Discussion:

Ask students:

- Did we learn anything about each other that we didn't already know? Were there any surprises?

✓ Safety Check

Have students remember to walk between groups.

💡 Tips and Comments

- *Have students talk about their answers when they are in their small groups.*
- *Feel free to ask clarifying questions to each group.*
- *Create questions that are both fun and meaningful. Some examples are listed below.*
- *Sample Questions:*
    1. *How many siblings in your family, including yourself?*
    2. *What is your favorite soft drink?*
    3. *What is your favorite out-of-school pastime?*
    4. *Who is your favorite music group?*
    5. *What do you like the most about our school?*
    6. *What do you dislike about phys. ed.?*
    7. *If you could change one thing about school, what would it be?*
    8. *What is your favorite color?*
    9. *If you could own any car, what would it be?*
    10. *What do you most want to learn in this class?*

Peek-a-Who

🕐 Estimated Time

25 minutes

Setup:

Ask two participants to hold the tarp or sheet between them. It should create a vertical barrier that can be raised and lowered easily. Divide the rest of the class into two groups, one on each side of the screen. Each group should sit on the ground.

Framing:

Say to students, "I know that most of you know each other's names. This game will test how many names you actually do know! The object of the game is to get people from the other team onto your team."

Procedure:

1. Ask one volunteer from each team to sit directly in front of their side of the screen. They need to do this quietly. When the screen is dropped, the two players must verbally identify each other by name. Whoever first identifies the

other person correctly wins. The slower player moves over to the faster person's team. Only permit the two volunteers to speak; the rest of the players must remain silent.

2. Asking groups of two, three or even four people to sit in front of the screen at the same time can vary rounds. It is always the fastest team that gets to bring people to their side.

3. The activity ends when there is only one large team!

Discussion:

Ask students:

- How did it feel to have to change teams? Did your allegiance change?
- Does everyone know each other's name? If not, fill in your "gaps."

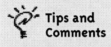 **Tips and Comments**

Additional variations include having people sit with their backs turned to the screen. Allow the rest of the class to give hints to the volunteers in front of the screen. Hints should be limited to describing the opposing player at the screen using positive descriptors of that person, such as, "She is a good listener." Be sure that the class is ready to limit themselves to positive rather than negative descriptors.

ASSESSMENT OPTION

A student's knowledge of his or her own self-esteem can be very enlightening. Adventure activities often bring self-esteem issues to light. Use the Self-Esteem Self-Assessment tool provided in the Assessment section near the end of this book to give students an opportunity for this personal evaluation. This tool can be used later in the curriculum to evaluate whether there have been any significant changes.

Section 2: Establishing Full Value Norms

In this lesson, students will participate in a problem-solving activity that they have already experienced in the sixth grade. In some ways it is a review; however, the activity requires group coordination each time it is done, making it a powerful lead-up to creating a Full Value Contract. The remainder of the lesson is the development of this class's Full Value Contract.

8.2.1

LESSON 1

Activities
- Turnstile
- The Village

Lesson Objectives
Students will be able to:
- Understand the importance of a Full Value Contract
- Demonstrate respectful behaviors toward self, peers and adults
- Demonstrate behaviors that are consistent with the Full Value Contract

Materials
- Jumping rope, about 50' long
- Markers and large flipchart paper

ACTIVITIES

Turnstile

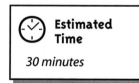

Estimated Time

30 minutes

Setup:
Select an additional rope turner to assist you. Ask the rest of the class to stand on one side of the jump rope. Begin turning.

Framing:
Say to students, "This activity requires the entire class to participate both in solving the problem and in implementing the solution. The task is simple: *Everyone* must get through the turning rope." Remind students of the Full Value Contract that they have used in the past; they should keep those behaviors in mind during the activity.

✓ Safety Check

- *If a player touches the rope, the rope turners should stop turning to avoid tripping or other injuries.*

- *Diving through the rope is not allowed.*

- *Be sure that the ground is even.*

Procedure:

Rules are:

- One person at a time in the rope-jumping area.

- Each player must make one jump through the turning rope.

- No missing a beat (no having the rope turn without a jumper jumping).

- If anyone misses, the entire class begins again.

- If the class is able and/or recalls this from sixth grade, you may start with some of the variations listed in Tips and Comments below.

- The initiative continues until the entire class has gone through the rope. If a rule is broken, the entire class begins again.

Discussion:

Ask students:

- What behaviors made the class successful during this activity? [Record these on flipchart paper.]

- Were there any behaviors that inhibited success? [Record these on flipchart paper.]

- Use these behaviors to start creating the Village [see next activity].

> **Tips and Comments**
>
> *• You can require students to jump in groups of two, three or four at a time. You can also have them come back through the rope the other way (thus experiencing the jump from the opposite angle), or invent alternative requirements of your own.*

. . . .

⏱ Estimated Time

30 minutes

The Village

Setup:

Have markers and flipchart paper available. You may want to have drawn a Village for the class prior to this point, but we usually recommend that you allow the students to do their own "art."

Framing:

Say to students, "We have been creating Full Value Contracts every year in physical education class. Can anyone explain to the class what purpose it serves and what it means? How does it help a class? Today we are going to create our FVC using a Village as our symbol. Can anyone try to explain why we would use a Village?"

Procedure:

1. Ask students to use the lists that were created during the Turnstile activity—the lists of behaviors that the class has already experienced and that they either like or don't like to have present.

2. Tell them that behaviors they want to keep should be written inside the Village; those they don't want to keep should be written outside the Village.

3. If the class is large, two groups can do this separately and then combine Villages to create one final contract.

4. The class is also free to create a mascot for their Village school, town landmarks, etc. Creativity is a wonderful thing.

Discussion:

Ask students:

- How do we know when our Full Value Contract is not being considered or when a negative behavior is present? What do we do about that?

- What can we do to keep this contract present and working?

- If conflict does arise, what should we do? Can we all agree to that?

Safety Check

- *Consider students' emotional safety when doing this activity.*

- *Work to draw out everyone's voice. Also be alert for examples of negative behavior that may be too directed.*

Tips and Comments

- *Allow for a thorough discussion following this initiative. It is time well spent.*

8.2.2

LESSON 2

This lesson gives the class an enjoyable review of their new Full Value Contract. It then gives them an opportunity to put the contract into practice.

> ### Activities
> - Full Value Speed Rabbit
> - Group Juggle
>
> ### Lesson Objectives
> Students will be able to:
> - Set achievable personal goals that can be self-assessed
> - Apply techniques for maintaining the FVC
> - Use the FVC effectively to manage conflict in the group
>
> ### Materials
> - Tape and markers
> - Soft throwable balls—a handful more than there are students in the class

ACTIVITIES

Full Value Speed Rabbit

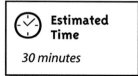

Estimated Time

30 minutes

Setup:
Ask the class to stand in a circle, shoulder to shoulder. Remind them that they have played this before in an earlier grade. Students like this activity! Have fun with the demonstration if students don't remember the game. You will set the tone of this initiative.

Framing:
Review the Village that students created in the last lesson. Have it displayed for them to see. Explain to the class, "We will be playing a game using some of the Full Value Contract components that you put into your Village."

Procedure:
1. Have the class develop human "statues" or symbols that represent some of their key Full Value components. These symbols will be made up of three people each. Have students practice forming the various symbols. (See #5 on the following page for symbol ideas.)

2. Choose one person to be in the center of the circle (the leader). The leader turns around and around, then randomly points to someone in the circle and calls out a symbol or Full Value component. The leader counts to 10.

3. The player who is pointed to becomes the main body of the statue. The people who are on either side of this player become the two sides. They must try to form themselves into the statue before the leader finishes counting. If they don't, the part of the symbol that is not in place by the count of 10 takes the leader's spot in the middle. If they are done in time, the leader stays put.

4. As the class masters the different symbols, add animals and other creative statues to the game.

5. Symbol or statue ideas:

    Be Here: Center person stands in a sumo wrestler stance, with hands on hips. Side people each grab one of the center person's arms and pull, showing that the center person is "here."

    Be Safe: Center person waves a baseball "safe" sign, while the sides each put a leg into the middle as if sliding into base.

    Let Go and Move On: Center person turns his or her back, while the side people pretend to be letting go of a rope that they have been pulling on.

    Elephant: Center person extends left arm down and holds nose with right hand to form a trunk. Side people form ears by facing the center person and making a C shape with their arms.

    Rabbit: Center person uses hands to make rabbit ears on his or her head. Sides each stand near the center person while making fast kicking/stepping motions with their legs like a rabbit.

Discussion:

Have the class split into small groups. Ask each group to discuss one of the Full Value components. Individual groups should answer the question, "How will we know when we are doing our Full Value component and when we are not?" Have each group report out to the class.

 **Tips and Comments**

• *Keep the game fun!*

• *Add all sorts of variations to the statues/symbols, and don't forget to let the class create their own*

ASSESSMENT OPTION

After this series of lessons, use the Compassion—Peer Assessment tool provided in this volume. Compassion is an important component of the Full Value Contract, and receiving peer feedback can be invaluable. Remember that peer assessment does not have to be used as an evaluation tool that affects a student's overall grade. Use this tool wisely. See the Assessment section near the end of this book.

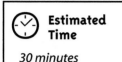

Estimated Time

30 minutes

✓ **Safety Check**

Make sure that the balls are soft and that rambunctious throws are discouraged.

Group Juggle

Setup:

1. Split the class up into groups of about 10 each.
2. Give each group a roll of tape and a few markers.
3. Keep the balls until you have finished briefing the class to prevent an immediate breach of the FVC!!

Framing:

Say to students, "We are going to do an activity that will bring to life our FVC concepts and norms. To start, each of you should write, on a piece of tape, one Full Value norm that you feel is very important, or one that you feel may be difficult to follow. I am going to give each of you a ball to tape your norm onto. This activity will require us to effectively juggle our norms!"

Procedure:

1. Starting with one ball per group, have each group develop a throwing pattern following these guidelines:
   • You cannot throw to someone on your immediate right or left.
   • You can only throw and catch once each while developing your pattern.
   • Once everyone has thrown once and caught the ball once, make sure that the pattern can be recreated.
   • Practice the pattern a number of times.
2. You may ask the group to set a goal regarding how many balls they think they can juggle at once.
3. Students will now attempt to juggle as many of these norms as possible without dropping any. Start each group with just a few balls, and gradually add more.
4. An amazing performance would be for a group to juggle one more ball than there are people in the group!

Discussion:

Ask students:
   • What happened when a ball was dropped?
   • Is this similar to what we may do when we "drop" a Full Value norm?
   • Was it difficult to juggle multiple balls? Might it be hard to juggle multiple norms?
   • Do we feel confident that we can manage our FVC?

> 🔦 **Tips and Comments**
>
> *•A negative norm can be added to each group; this ball should be required to go in reverse direction!*
>
> *•The discussion for this variation could focus on what occurs when we focus on negative norms versus positive norms.*

Section 3: Problem Solving

This is an excellent introductory initiative. Students will be challenged to think creatively and to react to a changing environment.

LESSON 1

Activities
- Change Up
- Overhand Knot

Lesson Objectives
Students will be able to:
- Work together to achieve common goals
- Apply effective problem-solving strategies to accomplish group tasks
- Be open to using a variety of ideas in the problem-solving process

Materials
- A set of laminated numbers that equal the number of students in the class (with classes over 30, multiple sets of numbers are needed) OR
- A deck of cards, substituted for the laminated numbers
- A piece of play rope or 9-mm rope, about 6' long.
- Extra pieces of rope for knot-tying practice

ACTIVITIES

Change Up

Setup:
None needed.

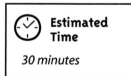

Estimated Time

30 minutes

Framing:

1. Say to students, "This activity explores dealing with changes. Each of you will be given a card. Please do not turn it over and look at it until you are told to do so.

2. "Your group will be given a series of challenges. After each challenge is identified, you will have several opportunities to plan and find solutions. Your group's goal is to execute the solution as efficiently and quickly as possible. Once you have had a chance to improve on your solution, a new challenge will

be presented. The goal will be to be just as efficient with each new challenge and each solution."

3. With a large class, have multiple groups of at least 15 doing the same task side by side. You can brief them as one class all trying to achieve world record times collectively. This allows for collaboration versus competition between groups.

Procedure:

1. Hand out a card to each person. Students cannot look at their cards until you tell them to.

2. Remind students that they will be timed on their execution of their group's solution. Tell groups that they must signal you once they have finished the task so that you stop timing them.

3. Give everyone **Challenge #1:** "Turn your cards over. Now line yourselves up *in numerical order,* from smallest to largest card number."

4. After they finish, tell each group their time on this attempt. This time represents their first benchmark.

5. Ask groups to shuffle their cards by having each person trade cards at least three times with someone different. Once they get a new card to keep, students must refrain from looking until they are told to do so. Give them a few minutes of planning time to refine their solution to Challenge #1.

6. Give the start signal and time the second solution. Report these times to the groups.

7. Allow one or two more attempts until you think students have achieved good times. Make sure that they shuffle the cards after each attempt.

8. Make a change by announcing **Challenge #2:** "Line yourselves up *alphabetically* now, according to the first letter of the number on your card. Say "Start," and time the attempts.

9. Report times to the groups, then repeat rules 5–7 as appropriate.

10. Make another change by announcing **Challenge #3:** "Now line up in two lines: odd numbers in one line, even numbers in the other. The odds should be in descending order, and evens should be in ascending numerical order."

11. Report times to the groups, then repeat rules 5-7 as appropriate.

Discussion:

Ask students:

- What were some consequences of change during this activity? Was it different if the changes were "minor" (for example, shuffling the cards, but still using the same numbers) or "major" (like changing from lining up numerically to lining up alphabetically)?

- Did you manage to develop solutions to each major change that produced significant improvements in your time? How?

- What strategies did you develop to adjust to change? What worked and what didn't?

- What can we learn about managing change in our own lives?

Overhand Knot

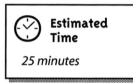

Estimated Time

25 minutes

Setup:

Hand out scrap play ropes or 9mm rope. Quickly show students how to tie an overhand knot. (Entire class mastery is not critical at this time.) Once your demonstration is finished, gather up all of the ropes again.

Line the class up side by side. They should all be holding hands, except for the two students in the middle of the line, who are given a rope to hold instead.

Framing:

Say to students, "Now we are going to tie one overhand knot as an entire class."

Procedure:

1. Reiterate to the group that their challenge is to tie an overhand knot in the middle of the rope that is being held by the two middle students.
2. The two students who are holding the rope must continue to hold it with one whole hand each until the activity is over.
3. The rest of the class also needs to continue holding hands.
4. The initiative is solved when the group has tied an overhand knot in the middle of the rope!

Discussion:

Ask students:

• What were the problem-solving strategies that the group used to tie the knot?
• How did being in a line affect your ability to communicate?
• Was the task easier or harder than it sounded? Why or why not?

LESSON 2

This lesson will give students a chance to truly think "out of the box." It also gives the class a chance to refine skills through practice and problem solving.

Activities
- Mergers
- Pipeline

Lesson Objectives
Students will be able to:

- Work together to achieve common goals
- Apply effective problem-solving strategies to accomplish group tasks
- Be open to using a variety of ideas in the process of solving problems
- Implement positive mechanisms to deal with and learn from failure
- Evaluate the effectiveness of their problem-solving process and solutions, and implement necessary changes to make them work better

Materials:

- Set of Merger ropes (thin ropes tied in loops of varying sizes, from small enough to fit only one pair of feet to one large enough for the entire class to get their feet in while sitting down)
- Pipeline set, obtainable through Project Adventure

ACTIVITIES

Mergers

Estimated Time

30 minutes

Setup:
Have each student take a rope, place it on the floor, and stand in the loop.

Framing:
Say to the class, "As you know, school requires you to deal with change all of the time. It's important that each of you finds a safe way to manage this change. In this activity, safety is represented by having each of you positioned with both feet inside a loop."

Procedure:

1. Say to students, "When I say, 'Change,' each of you must leave the loop you are in and find a new 'safe place.' Remember, safety means both feet completely in a loop."

2. After each "change," remove some loops. Eventually leave the class with one large loop to keep everyone safe. (Usually students do not ask how they can change loops if there is only one left, but if they do, explain that this change requires adapting to the additional people joining them.)

3. The solution is for students to change the original paradigm (needing to stand inside the loop) to a new one (sitting outside the loop with both feet in the middle).

Discussion:

Ask students:

- Were you ever worried about not finding a safe place for yourself? Did you worry about others finding a safe place?
- How did the class share ideas? Where did the final solution come from?
- How can this class continue to be safe for everyone?
- Did you remember the ABCDE's of Problem Solving from last year?

Safety Check

- *Make sure that the ground is even and that students don't push each other when moving from loop to loop.*

- *Do not allow students' final solution to involve getting onto each other's backs. When (if) they start to do this, tell them it is not allowed and that there are other options.*

Tips and Comments

Let the students solve the problem themselves. They will get it!

Pipeline

Setup:

Create a zone or path that is a number of steps longer than the number of people in the class (or in each group). At the end of the zone, place a bucket or container. If the class is larger than 15, it is best to do this in multiple groups. The groups can be positioned to work side by side, or in a passing format.

Give each student a pipe. Give each group a series of objects that come with the Pipeline set.

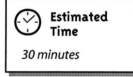

Estimated Time

30 minutes

Framing:

1. Say to students, "You are all working for a company that is trying to produce as many items as it can. In order for the product to be ready for shipment, it must pass through the full pipeline, which ends in the final container."

2. Now say, "Before you begin, you may practice behind the start line for five minutes. At that time, I would like you to set an aggressive but attainable goal. You will have 20 minutes to execute and meet your goal. Listen carefully to the procedures and rules of the activity before setting your goal."

Safety Check

Be careful of fallen marbles on the floor.

Procedure:

1. Only one person can touch the object, and that is at the start of the pipeline behind the start line.
2. The object must never stop moving when it is in the pipeline, and it can never move backwards.
3. If the object is in a student's pipe, that student may not move his or her feet.
4. Pipes cannot touch each other.
5. If any of the above occur, production stops, and every object in the pipeline goes back to the starting area. Products that have made it to shipping (the container) may remain there.
6. If an object drops, it goes back to the start.

Discussion:

Ask students:

- How did the group use the different strengths of class members?
- How did you manage failure? When rules were broken?
- Were you able to adapt to different objects?
- Are you content with the number of objects you brought to shipment?

> **Tips and Comments**
>
> • *You can make this more difficult by putting obstacles and bends in the pipeline pathway.*
> • *Handing your group a written copy of the rules can help them plan more effectively.*

This is an interesting group task that involves students finding solutions and then coordinating their group.

Activity
- The Meuse

Lesson Objectives
Students will be able to:
- Apply effective problem-solving strategies to accomplish group tasks
- Be open to using a variety of ideas in the process of solving problems
- Use the different strengths of individuals in the group
- Evaluate the effectiveness of their problem-solving process, and implement necessary changes to make it work better
- Establish procedures that are safe and effective for the given task
- Use roles of leadership and followership in accomplishing group tasks

Materials
- 8 cinder blocks or other sturdy blocks
- 4 boards, 4" x 4" x 8'
- 12' section of 9-mm rope

ACTIVITY

The Meuse

Setup:
The placement of the blocks and the length of the boards are both critical factors in the success of this activity. Make sure the blocks are placed far enough apart so that a board will not reach diagonally from one block to another (see diagram on the following page). The solution to this activity is shown in the diagram: students place the boards in a T formation so that they can reach a forward block without having to place a board diagonally (which is not possible if the correct setup is used).

Students are asked to stand behind the two starting blocks while they are given the framing and the procedures. The boards are given to the students while they are still in the starting area.

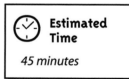

Estimated
Time

45 minutes

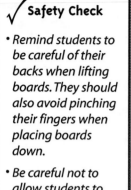

Safety Check

• *Remind students to be careful of their backs when lifting boards. They should also avoid pinching their fingers when placing boards down.*

• *Be careful not to allow students to jump onto the blocks.*

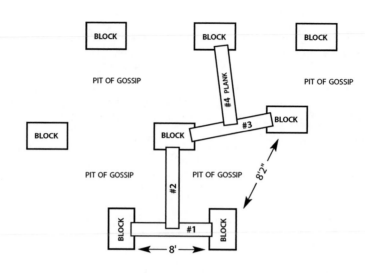

Framing:

Say to students, "The entire class must cross the big pit below the boards. It is called the Pit of Gossip. At the other end is the Area of Clear Communication. The tools that you will be able to use include everyone in the group; the cinder blocks, which can't be moved; these four boards; and this rope."

Procedure:

1. No one can touch the ground.
2. No board can touch the ground.
3. Everyone must get from one side to the other.

Discussion:

Ask students:

• What were the elements of clear communication that the class used?
• Were those who "followed" during the activity able to stay engaged?
• Were you able to be safe?
• Is gossiping a problem at school?
• What can we do to minimize gossiping in school?

 **Tips and Comments**

Check your setup to be sure that the boards cannot reach from one cinder block to another on the diagonal.

ASSESSMENT OPTION

How is the sense of community in this class? Is it healthy? Is it what students want it to be? The Student Community Survey, found in the Assessment section near the end of this book, gives students a chance to evaluate their community using their own survey questions. This is a fun tool. This type of assessment can easily be integrated into a math project as well.

Section 4: Building Trust

8.4.1

LESSON 1

This lesson is a trust sequence—a series of activities with increasing levels of commitment being asked of the students. This is a powerful sequence that touches on the Full Value Contract and Challenge by Choice and also teaches spotting.

Activities

- Trust Lean
- Three-Person Lean
- Wind in the Willow
- Levitation

Lesson Objectives

Students will be able to:

- Apply Challenge by Choice to risk-taking situations
- Be reliable members of the group by offering each other physical and emotional support
- Demonstrate how progressive personal challenges, within a safe environment, can lead to increased self-awareness and learning opportunities
- Express their emotions in a supportive environment
- Respect and support their own and others' decisions
- Use the FVC as a tool to manage potential breakdowns in trust

Materials

None needed

ACTIVITIES

Trust Lean

Setup:

Have the class split into pairs.

Framing:

Say to students, "This is an opportunity to learn and practice correct spotting technique. It is also an opportunity to develop trust between you and your classmates. Do we all have someone that we lean on for support? What is it about that

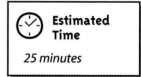

Estimated Time

25 minutes

Safety Check

• *Make sure that you have proper training before doing this sequence.*

• *You may need to add student names to the fall signals so groups don't get their communications mixed up.*

• *It is OK to have different-sized people working together, within reason.*

• *Make sure that the ground is level and clear.*

• *Assess your class's readiness for this activity before beginning.*

person that allows us to do that? As spotters today, you will each have a chance to be that person who is literally being leaned on for support."

Procedure:

1. Demonstrate each step of the sequence, asking a student to be the leaner/faller so that you can teach proper spotting.

2. Ask the faller to stand with arms crossed in front of his or her chest, keeping elbows from flying out. The faller must also keep feet still and body stiff.

3. The spotter stands about a foot behind the leaner/faller, with one foot in front of the other. The spotter's knees are bent, and arms and hands are up. This is the proper spotting stance.

4. Make sure that the class understands the concept of spotting. The critical area to protect is the head, neck and back of the faller. This may mean that you can only break a fall rather than actually catch a fall.

5. The object of the activity is for the leaner/faller to fall backward against the spotter's hands. The spotter then pushes the faller back to an upright stance.

6. Verbal communication is critical here:

   Faller: "Are you ready to catch?"

   Spotter: "Ready to catch."

   Faller: "Leaning."

   Spotter: "OK, lean."

7. After each fall, the spotter can ask if the faller would like to step farther away.

8. Remind the class that this is not the place for joking around. Not catching someone is absolutely not allowed. This is a serious trust-building activity.

Discussion:

Ask students:

• What was it like to be the faller? What was it like to be the spotter?

• Did you prefer one role over the other?

• Was a level of trust established? How?

Tips and Comments

• *You cannot overemphasize the need for all students to pay close attention during this activity.*

• *Make sure that there is clear communication about when the activity is over. We suggest the spotter putting both hands on the faller's shoulders to designate that they have completed that series of falls.*

Three-Person Lean

Setup:
Have students form groups of three.

Framing:
Say to students, "This activity is very similar to the Trust Lean, but it involves two spotters so that the faller can go both forward and back! Please keep in mind all that you learned in the last exercise about trust and challenge."

Procedure:
1. Once again demonstrate, with you acting as one of the spotters.
2. Ask the faller to use the same posture and arm position as in the Trust Lean.
3. Both spotters should stand equidistantly from the faller—only a short step away to begin with.
4. Establish with the group that the first lean will always be forward.
5. The faller initiates communication, as in the Trust Lean. Both spotters need to respond with "Ready."
6. When the communication sequence has been completed, the spotters gently pass the faller back and forth between them. It is important to emphasize a slow and gentle pace!

Discussion:
Use the Full Value Contract as the basis for a short discussion about how the activity has gone for each trio.

Estimated Time

25 minutes

Safety Check

• *The same issues apply here as for the Trust Lean.*

• *Be sure that spotters don't pass the faller aggressively back and forth.*

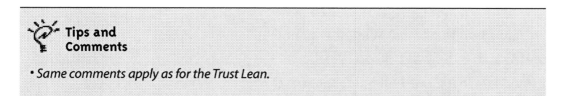

Tips and Comments

• *Same comments apply as for the Trust Lean.*

Estimated Time

35 minutes

Safety Check

- *Challenge by Choice is essential in this activity.*

- *12–15 people is the maximum number for each group so that the circle does not get too large.*

Wind in the Willow

Setup:
Have the class divide up into groups of 8 to 10. Members of each group should stand in a circle.

Framing:
Say to students, "Because you have done so well in these introductory leans, we are ready for the next level of challenge. During this activity you, as the faller, will need to establish trust between yourself and all the members of your group."

Procedure:

1. Have the class observe one group while you demonstrate.
2. Ask a volunteer to stand in the middle. This person, as the faller, must do everything that the faller did in the leaning activities: arms crossed across the chest, feet planted solidly on the ground, body stiff.
3. The spotters around the circle need to stand close together, shoulder to shoulder. There should be no gaps in the circle where the faller could slip through.
4. The group should use the same commands as those used in the leans.
5. This time, the faller may fall in any direction. The group is to pass the faller gently around in a random pattern.
6. Stress that no one person should ever be the only one holding the faller; there should always be multiple people with hands on the faller.

Discussion:
Ask students:

- Was it harder to trust the larger group in this activity than the smaller groups in the Leans? Why or why not?
- As a class, how did we do overall?
- Are we living our Full Value Contract?
- Are we ready to go to the next level of challenge?

Tips and Comments

You may ask students to be silent while a person is being passed around. This can help maintain emotional safety by reducing unwanted comments.

Levitation

Setup:
Keep the same groups, or at least the same group sizes, as you did for Wind in the Willow.

Framing:
Ask the class, "Does everyone know what levitation is? Well, today we will all get a chance to experience it if we choose."

Procedure:

1. Ask for a volunteer to lie on the ground, face up.

2. The rest of the group should place their hands under the volunteer's body. Someone should tend exclusively to the person's head.

3. Pick a leader (who should be you for the first round). The leader is the voice who calls out the commands for each round of the activity. The leader asks if the volunteer is ready. If the volunteer answers "Yes," then the leader asks, "Lifters ready?" The group responds accordingly.

4. When everyone is ready, on the leaders count, the group lifts the volunteer to waist level. It is important that the volunteer remain very stiff and still.

5. Depending on the group and the comfort of the volunteer, he or she can be raised higher, even going as high as head level.

6. On the leader's count, the volunteer is then slowly lowered, with a gentle rocking motion added to the descent, until he or she is safely on the ground.

Discussion:
Have a discussion after this activity that flows naturally from the other discussions that have occurred during this trust sequence. Highlight important themes that have emerged, and ask further questions where appropriate.

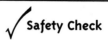

Safety Check

- *The same safety issues apply here as in the rest of the sequence.*

- *Make sure that the volunteer's head stays even with the rest of his or her body and that the body stays level.*

- *Remind people that a person's torso is heavier than the legs. Position more people to lift in the torso area.*

Tips and Comments

- *Only let the group lift the volunteer higher if she or he gives permission to do so.*

- *You may have the group turn in a 360° circle after the person is raised.*

- *Ask the person being lifted to close his or her eyes.*

- *Doing this in silence makes for a very peaceful experience.*

- *Levitation can be combined with Wind in the Willow. Designate a person in the Wind in the Willow circle who will be the head person for the levitation. After the volunteer in the middle has been passed around the circle a few times, the group should lean the volunteer toward the head person. Everyone should then gently lower the volunteer into a levitation position. The volunteer will not ever lie on the ground, but rather should be lowered into the arms of the people in the circle and then picked up entirely. Then levitation continues as already described.*

Section 5: Experiences Using Low Elements

LESSON 1

This is a swing activity that is more complex than the Nitro Crossing activity done in Grade 6. This activity allows students to apply what they have previously learned to a new situation.

Activity
- Disc Jockeys

Lesson Objectives
Students will be able to:
- Physically challenge themselves in a safe environment
- Appropriately apply their own strengths and recognize their own weaknesses
- Respect others' different strengths and weaknesses
- Rely on their group to support positive risk taking
- Recognize when fatigue can lead to injury

Materials
- Swing rope, obtainable through Project Adventure
- Hula Hoops—enough so that all participants can be accommodated inside them as the hoops lie on the ground

ACTIVITY

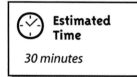

Estimated Time

30 minutes

Disc Jockeys

Setup:
Be sure that the swing rope is properly attached and installed. Place a series of Hula Hoops at the end of the swing area. These will serve as targets to land in. Be sure to space the hoops out so that landing from the rope is challenging, or else the activity will look a lot like Nitro Crossing.

Framing:
Say to students, "In order for this class to advance to a world where everyone's differences are embraced, first you have to travel across the Sea of Prejudice and land

in the Sphere of Acceptance. As you do this activity, be sure to embrace the differences that exist in this group."

Procedure:

1. After the start line, no one is allowed to touch the Sea of Prejudice (the ground below the entire swing area) unless they are inside a hoop.

2. Everyone must start over if someone touches the ground.

3. The rope should be hung in the middle of the swing area!

4. More than one person can be in a hoop at one time.

5. Every hoop needs to have at least one person in it before the activity is complete.

6. Students cannot move from hoop to hoop once they have landed.

7. Make sure that people are spotted at the start and finish of their swings.

8. When and if the person swinging lets go with his or her hands, the swinger's feet must be completely out of the loop in the rope.

9. No wild swinging or kicking allowed when students are landing inside a hoop.

Discussion:

Ask students:

- Did the class value the differences that exist here?

- Did the solution involve everyone?

- As people got tired of swinging, were they able to ask for help?

- Did the class show compassion to those who had a more difficult time swinging?

- How does this class value differences outside of physical education class? How are differences valued socially? Sit with a partner, and discuss examples of when differences have been valued and when they have not been valued outside this class.

Tips and Comments

Remember not to make this too easy for students by placing the hoops too close to the end of the swing area!

Safety Check

- *Follow spotting procedures as stated in the Project Adventure Safety Manual or as learned in your training.*

- *Make sure that the ground and area above the swing are free of obstructions.*

- *Make sure that the rope is properly secured.*

- *Give students a chance to practice some swinging before the initiative starts. This takes the pressure off people who may have trouble swinging.*

- *Teachers may need to spot students as they swing.*

- *Instruct students to swing gently and not kick their feet if they are near other people.*

- *If students are going to let go of the swing rope, they must put a foot down and stop their swing.*

LESSON 2

This is a low-element activity that can keep the entire group active for most of the class period. The difficulty of communicating while standing in a line increases the problem-solving nature of the activity.

Activity
- Mohawk Walk

Lesson Objectives
Students will be able to:
- Physically challenge themselves in a safe environment
- Appropriately apply their own strengths and recognize their own weaknesses
- Respect others' different strengths and weaknesses
- Rely on their group to support positive risk taking
- Recognize when fatigue can lead to injury
- Apply proper spotting technique

Materials
- Mohawk Walk low element, obtainable through Project Adventure

ACTIVITY

Mohawk Walk

Estimated Time

45 minutes

Setup:
Check to make sure that the Mohawk Walk has been properly set up. Review spotting prior to this activity.

Framing:
Say to students, "You all have the rest of the school year to get through, both in this class and in others. In order for each of you to get what you want from this year, you have to support each other's efforts and goals. This series of cables represents the rest of the year. If you all make it to the end, all of your goals will be met."

Procedure:
1. Once someone is on a cable, it is not permitted to touch the ground unless that person is needed for spotting.

2. No one is allowed to traverse on the cables solo.

3. No running on the cable or diving for a tree or post.

4. Spotters are necessary if the class cannot control its movement on the cable, if a participant asks to be spotted, or when it appears that someone needs to step off. Spotters are not mandatory throughout the activity, however. Use your professional discretion.

5. Any participant who feels that he or she is going to fall off of a cable should step off before taking anyone else along.

6. If anyone does step off, this person needs to return back to the start of the last completed leg of the traverse.

7. Remind the class of proper spotting techniques if spotting becomes necessary.

Discussion:

Ask students:

- Did everyone make it to the end of the school year (end of the cable series) with their goals met?

- What was needed for this to occur?

- How were you able to communicate with each other once you were all on the cable? Is this similar to what needs to occur at times in the "real world"?

- What can we take from today to help us all get along for the rest of the year?

Safety Check

- *Follow spotting procedures as stated in the Project Adventure Safety Manual or as learned in your training.*

- *Emphasize stepping off the cable before pulling others off, too.*

- *Some class behaviors may require spotting for every participant. If this is the case, once someone reaches a tree, he or she is to step off and spot others.*

- *No running on the cables.*

Tips and Comments

- *You can add a prop (such as a crutch) to aid the class over difficult sections.*

- *You can ask the group to carry an object with them that represents something relevant.*

- *Rather than having students go back to the previous leg when they step off, you can have*

ASSESSMENT OPTION

Evaluate the class's problem-solving ability using the Problem Solving—Group Assessment checklist, provided in the Assessment section that follows. This can be used to assess multiple lessons or to assess an individual lesson.

LESSON 3

This low-element activity is more of an individual challenge, requiring the support of others, and less of a problem-solving activity. It offers a wonderful way for students to explore ways of moving that they may not have attempted before.

Activity
- Low Climbing Wall Traverse

Lesson Objectives
Students will be able to:
- Apply proper spotting techniques to appropriate situations
- Physically challenge themselves in a safe environment
- Appropriately apply their own strengths and recognize their own weaknesses
- Respect others' different strengths and weaknesses
- Rely on their group to support positive risk taking
- Recognize when fatigue can lead to injury

Materials
- Properly installed low climbing traverse, obtainable through Project Adventure

ACTIVITY

Estimated Time

45 minutes

Low Climbing Wall Traverse

Setup:
None needed. You may want to split the class into groups of three, depending on how you frame the activity.

Framing:
Say to students, "This is a chance to do some individual goal setting and risk taking while being supported by your classmates. I ask that each of you challenge your concept of moving—from walking or running to climbing or traversing, using good climbing technique and thoughtful movements. Once you have practiced on the wall for a few attempts, each of you can set goals as to how far you think you can traverse without falling off."

Teach the class some basic climbing techniques. These can include the following key principles:
- Using one's feet, looking down more than looking up
- Staying in balance, keeping weight in and over one's feet
- Moving with intention, planning ahead

- Weight shifts—how to make them and what they can do for the climber
- Different grip techniques

Review basic spotting techniques with the class if necessary.

Procedure:

1. If students are grouped in threesomes, have one member of each group climb while the other two spot. (This can be done one on one, but with larger classes threesomes help to keep everyone involved.)

2. We usually suggest that students be given some "free" climbing time to explore the techniques listed above. How this is structured depends on the length of the wall, but having multiple students on at one time is fine as long as they are acting as responsible spotters.

3. After students have had an opportunity to practice, allow them to do some personal goal setting as to how far they think they can traverse the wall without falling.

4. Challenges can be set up between partners if appropriate. This can include partners selecting a series of holds that each person should use, and then both partners attempting this series in turn.

5. Be creative, using variations on how this activity is set up for students. If they are given proper time to practice and enough wall space to climb on, a low traverse can be an element used for multiple days—and multiple years.

Discussion:

Ask students:

- In your groups, discuss how well each of you felt supported by the others. What did you learn about climbing while watching each other? Were there some things that your partner(s) did better than you?

- As a class, discuss the notion of safety. Was this a safe environment in which to challenge yourself?

- What kind of challenge did you set for yourself? Was it hard enough, too hard, or not hard enough? Is this typical of other parts of your life?

Safety Check

- *Be sure that students are skilled in spotting before doing this activity. If not, reteach a spotting progression.*

- *Make sure that the traverse does not allow students to climb too high. If there are holds that you feel are unsafe, draw a line over which feet are not allowed.*

- *Be sure that the landing area under the traverse is even and free of obstructions.*

Tips and Comments

- *As mentioned above, be creative on the variations that you use in this activity.*
- *Use tape to color-code interesting climbing options that have a variety of difficulty levels. (Put colored tape near every hold that can be used in a particular sequence.)*
- *This activity can also be used as a place for students to stay active during other activities that are better done with fewer people. Obviously, it still needs to be monitored properly.*

ASSESSMENT OPTION

The theme of respecting differences has been stressed throughout this unit. The Respect for Differences Rubric, in the Assessment section that follows, provides an excellent tool for evaluating students' ability to integrate this important concept into their behavior.

8.5.4

LESSON 4

This final low-element activity once again focuses on group participation and problem solving.

Activity
- Spider's Web: People Version

Lesson Objectives
Students will be able to:
- Apply proper spotting techniques to appropriate situations
- Appropriately apply their own strengths and recognize their own weaknesses
- Respect others' different strengths and weaknesses
- Rely on their group to support positive risk taking

Materials
- A portable or installed Spider's Web, obtainable through Project Adventure
- Index cards and pens

· ·

ACTIVITY

Estimated Time

35 minutes

Spider's Web: People Version

Setup:
If you are using a portable web, put it together and set it up at the location of the activity. Ask the class to stand on one side of the web.

Framing:
Say to students, "You are all standing on the side of the web that represents the current state of where you are in relation to this year at school. The other side of the web represents the completion of a specific goal that you have for this year. This is similar to the Mohawk Walk, but this time I want you to be specific about your goal. Before we begin the activity, which is to get everyone to the other side of the web, write one goal that you have for yourself for this school year. I will be asking you to share this goal with the class."

Procedure:

1. The task is to get the entire group to the other side.

2. Neither the web, nor any of the web standards, can be touched.

3. If a touch is made, everyone must start again. (Or, you may decide to just send back that individual plus two or three others, depending on how difficult you want to make this activity.)

4. No one is allowed to "dive" through the web.

5. A hole can only be used once. (If there are not enough holes for every student, you will need to specify how many holes can be used more than once.)

6. It is important that everyone support the goals of each person going through the web.

7. Before going through, each person must read aloud her or his goal for the year.

Discussion:

Ask students:

- Individually, each of you should consider your goal. Does it seem too hard, too easy, or just right?

- Did you feel as though the class supported you in this activity? Are there people who can support your goals at school?

- What seemed to work best for people during this activity? What might have been frustrating?

- What key points do we want to capture from today to bring to other aspects of this school year?

✓ Safety Check

- *Follow spotting procedures as stated in the Project Adventure Safety Manual or as learned in your training.*

- *Once again, be sure that students are comfortable and skilled at spotting.*

- *You may want to demonstrate proper lifting techniques. (Remind the class of the levitation exercise that they have done previously.)*

- *Be sure that students lower each other feet first.*

- *There must be active spotting during all lifts and passes.*

💡 Tips and Comments

- *Make sure that there are enough holes to accommodate very large students easily.*

- *If there are students who are very uncomfortable going through the web, you may need to give them a different option for getting to the other side.*

- *If for some reason the trust sequence in Section 4, Lesson 1, was not completed, do so before using the Spider's Web.*

- *For a single-sided web, 15 students is a workable number. With larger classes, either use two webs, or have half of the class on the low traverse or other self-spotting activity while the other half is engaged in this activity.*

8.5.4

FINAL LESSON

Final Lesson: Putting It All Together, Grade 8

This final lesson ends the Adventure unit for Grade 8. This lesson is designed to provide students with time to celebrate the goals they have achieved, the chance to reflect on lessons learned, and an opportunity to consider how to transfer this learning to the rest of the year and to their lives.

Activities

We suggest that you choose activities from the entire range of activities that have been done in this unit. Allowing class input as to what they would like to repeat for this final class can also be effective.

It is best to choose a variety of activities: some fun warmups, a couple of games that students have really enjoyed, some initiatives and low elements that they have done especially well, and even one or two that may have been challenging for them. The number of activities selected depends on the length of the lesson you are hoping to lead. This lesson can easily take more than one class period.

Lesson Objectives:
Students will be able to:

- Demonstrate respectful behaviors toward self, peers and adults
- Apply effective problem-solving strategies to accomplish group tasks
- Rely on the group to support appropriate risk taking
- Appropriately apply strengths and recognize weaknesses

Materials

- Dependent upon the activities selected
- Prewritten rules for each individual initiative that is selected

ACTIVITIES

Instructor's Choice *(see above)*

Estimated Time

60–120 minutes

Setup:
This lesson should be set up as a series of activities to be accomplished by the class. Arrange these initiatives and/or low elements in different locations that you can monitor. After some large-group warmups and games, you may have to divide the class into smaller groups for the initiatives.

Framing:

Say to students, "As a way to end our Adventure unit, we are going to have a second chance to do some of our favorite games and to complete some of our favorite and most challenging initiatives. The goal of this lesson is for the entire class to gain the largest number of points possible. Each small group will be gaining points for the whole class. Remember to apply all that you have learned. "

Procedure:

1. Do some favorite warmups and large-group games.

2. Split the class into groups. Start each group on a different initiative.

3. Hand out rule sheets, and remind each group of important safety considerations. Give rule clarification as needed.

4. Give each group a specific amount of time in which to complete an initiative.

5. Create a scoring system that gives the most points for full completion, fewer points for partial completion, and perhaps minimal points for exhibiting positive behaviors.

6. Each group needs to self-score and self-monitor rule infractions.

7. After time limits are up, the groups should rotate until students have had a chance to do each initiative.

8. Remind the class that they are all working toward the same ultimate goal.

9. If students ask if they can help other groups, let them—this means that they are learning how to collaborate!

Discussion:

Ask students:

- In this lesson, did we as a class demonstrate all that we have learned in our Adventure unit? What are the important things we have learned?

- What key things have we learned that we can we keep using during the rest of the school year?

- What key things have we learned that we can apply to our out-of-school lives?

Safety Check

- *Be sure that the class is ready to work independently on the activities you select.*

  NOTE: Be sure that you choose activities that can be self-managed by the students as there will be multiple groups working simultaneously. If your class cannot manage this, or you would like to choose activities that do require adult supervision, we recommend that you have additional teachers and/or parent volunteers serving as dependable spotters during this session.

- *Stop action, and subtract points, if safety procedures are not followed.*

Tips and Comments

- *Try to select initiatives that take about the same amount of time to complete.*
- *Avoid initiatives that have only one solution, such as Mergers.*
- *You may want to select an initiative that students have done in a previous year.*
- *If the initiative portion of this lesson takes more than one class, take notes on where each group is at the end of the first class. They can then resume from similar starting points when they meet again.*

Middle School

Assessment

As indicated in the Introduction to this program, assessment is a complex topic that touches on a variety of educational issues. One's own philosophy of assessment certainly informs the types of assessment that end up being integrated into one's curriculum. The assessment section in this book has not been included to answer the debate of whether grading students A-F enhances or diminishes overall learning. Nor does it suggest how your department should answer the global question of how to evaluate students' overall physical education requirements. However, as national and state standards become more prevalent in physical education, so do well—designed assessment tools to help us understand whether the standards that have been set are met. This curriculum offers guidelines and tools for assessing students in the Adventure program described in this volume. We hope that some of these suggestions can both inform your teaching and will be integrated into your existing assessment or evaluation criteria.

BASIC DEFINITIONS

The topic of assessment is so expansive that it is important for educators to agree on a common vocabulary. Following are some terms and definitions that will be used in this section.

> **Assessment:** Systematic data gathering, used to make inferences about student progress in achieving designated learning outcomes, based on various sources of evidence
>
> **Evaluation:** Judgment regarding the quality, value or worth of a student's work and/or performance based upon established criteria and on multiple sources of information—using alternative tools when assessing
>
> **Authentic assessment:** Any form of assessment that emphasizes validity, fairness and the enhancement of learning
>
> **Embedded assessment:** Assessing students while they are involved in the learning process

Adventure activities and experiential programs naturally incorporate frequent embedded assessments. While students are engaged in problem—solving activities, teachers are able to assess performance, evaluate the appropriateness of student behaviors in relation to safety, and predict whether students will be successful so that discussion questions can be framed accordingly. In fact, embedded assessment is usually more present in Adventure activities than in a traditional physical education curriculum, where the number of goals scored determines success.

What is often missing in Adventure programs, however, are authentic assessment tools. How can a teacher assess whether or not a student is actually learning to get along better with others? How does one know that an individual is respecting the differences in the class? Although there may not be a good written test that allows educators to objectively evaluate topics such as these (thankfully), there are authentic assessment tools available that can certainly help assess such characteristics in a group of students.

Which assessment tools are appropriate to use depends on a number of factors, which is why this curriculum does not specify which tools to use when. These factors include:

- Age of the students
- Resources available
- Amount of time available
- Level of evaluation desired
- What you are trying to assess

However, there are some cornerstones to assessment that need to be kept in mind regardless of which tool is used for what purpose.

GOALS

Throughout this curriculum—and throughout a student's educational experience—a variety of goals are being set. These goals may be student—driven, teacher—driven, even district—and/or state—driven. Regardless of where these goals are generated, they should form the basis of student assessment. Data must be collected to help teachers and administrators understand if these goals are being achieved. Moreover, within each goal, it is important to clarify the level of "knowing" expected. For example, there is a significant difference between being able to identify something versus being able to do something. The clearer the goal, the clearer the assessment objective.

In the program described here, the Learning Outcomes detailed in each lesson provide a solid framework for class goals as they pertain to specific activities. Some activities ask students to set goals for themselves, which also become relevant in the assessment process. As you read through the Learning Outcomes, it will become obvious that some goals are easier to assess than others. For example, if an outcome is, "Every student can identify each classmate by name," this is easy to assess quickly. If the outcome reads, "Students will understand the different strengths and weaknesses in the class," a rubric style of assessment—and significantly more time—may be appropriate.

GIVING FEEDBACK

Regardless of which tool is used, assessment should include giving feedback to students so that they can continue to learn. This feedback should encompass information on areas of strength as well as areas needing improvement. Adventure activities provide many opportunities for this feedback to occur, both from teachers and from peers. A process that incorporates feedback is so much more meaningful to students than being given letter grades with no explanation as to what the letter grades mean. All that students learn from this process is that they have received a *C,* for example, instead of an *A.* With feedback, students have a clear understanding of specific areas needing development and specific areas of strength from which they can grow. Be aware, though, that feedback needs to be approached carefully—with thorough consideration of what is being said and how it might be heard. You may want to conduct a short lesson on feedback before engaging students in any peer feedback sessions.

LEVEL OF ASSESSMENT

There are two key levels of assessment involved in the measurement of learning and growth: one for students and one for teachers. Student assessment is more prevalent and should focus on whether students have achieved the objectives of a particular lesson or unit. Did each student reach the desired level of understanding as set by both student and teacher?

Assessing the teacher involves assessing the effectiveness of the lesson implementation. Did the group have a chance to achieve the learning outcomes? Could the activity have been framed differently? Did the teacher use GRABBSS effectively in choosing what to do when?

Both of these assessment levels—student and teacher —— can be addressed in a self—assessment format, a peer assessment format or in a teacher/supervisor format. Be careful when using a peer assessment model as a grading tool. Parents expect that an adult will grade their child, so teacher assessment should be incorporated in the final peer—assessed grade. In fact, we believe that using a variety of formats and getting feedback from a variety of levels provides individuals with the most comprehensive picture of their progress.

AUTHENTIC ASSESSMENT TOOLS

A variety of assessment tools are described below for your review and consideration. In each case, basics of each tool are highlighted. At the end of this section, some examples of specific assessment options that can be used directly in this curriculum are included. We fully expect that in order for you to thoroughly assess your students in a way that meets the evaluation criteria of your school, you will take these options and create a "system" that meets your needs. Staff members at Project Adventure are available for consultation in this process as well.

Rubrics

Rubrics incorporate criteria and standards to be evaluated that students know about in advance. For example, a traditional assessment tool may rate a student on a scale of 1–4 in a particular skill area, yet the that rating criteria may never be explained to the student. A rubric, on the other hand, clarifies in detail the level of understanding or mastery that each number represents, and these numbers are applied to the specific area being assessed. An example of such a rubric follows.

SAMPLE SCORING RUBRIC

1 = Unable to perform the skill

2 = Able to perform the skill with difficulty

3 = Able to perform the skill well

4 = Able to perform the skill at an advanced level

Students are aware of these criteria while they engage in their activities. This enables them to understand what, in fact, the goals of each lesson are. Teacher expectations and goals are thus clarified.

Observation with Checklist

A good checklist is very similar to a rubric if it includes a clear structure outlining what is being evaluated and how. Once again, when shared with students ahead of time, checklists help them to understand their progress and set personal goals. Checklists and rubrics can also be used effectively as peer assessment tools.

Journals

Journals are a very common authentic assessment tool, as they provide students with a wonderful opportunity to reflect on particular events or classes. This reflection can be left as a free—form medium, where the goal is to see that students have reflected on key aspects of a class, or they can be structured, with guiding questions to be answered in a journal-like medium. These guiding questions can be quite broad and act merely as catalysts for reflection, such as, "I am proud of what I did when…" Allowing for some unstructured writing is recommended. The use in Adventure programs has proved to be very powerful.

Self—Assessment Questions or Worksheets

When your intent is to keep journals a free-form reflection tool for students, structured self-assessment questions can be introduced in the form of worksheets. These sheets should include a variety of components, including open-ended questions for students to answer as well as rubrics or checklist models requiring students to rate themselves.

Projects

The expression of what someone has learned can be captured powerfully in special projects. When given the opportunity to develop skits, create posters, make videos or use some other creative form to demonstrate their key learning points, students often shine. Students and teachers alike can be surprised and impressed by the depth of understanding that this type of assessment can exhibit. Obviously, such projects take time and commitment, but when appropriate, they can be outstanding.

Standardized Assessment Tools

Information is available about more formal assessment tools, including their reliability and validity coefficients and the populations for which they are normed. Such information can be found through the Buros Institute of Mental Measurements (www.unl.edu/buros).

Specific Assessment Tools Designed for this Curriculum (Grades 6–8)

The following tools can be used, as they are written, with this curriculum. However, there is plenty of flexibility allowed so that you can redesign these tools to meet any specific requirements that exist in your program. We have included tools for teachers to assess both individual students and whole classes, tools for peer assessment and tools for self-assessment. Also included in the lessons themselves are numerous suggested assessment opportunities.

Respect for Differences Rubric

	Unaware/Ignore (Level 1)	Aware/Accept (Level 2)	Incorporate (Level 3)
Ideas	Does not respond to what is said Verbally acknowledges what is said No verbal attention given Physically excludes others (turns back, walks away) No visual attention given Cuts other person(s) off Does not allow others "air time"	Verbally acknowledges what is said Makes direct or indirect statements (can be in agreement or disagreement) Physically acknowledges what is said (nods head) Visual attention given	Allows implementation of ideas Supports changes Encourages contributions from others Integrates self into group process
Decisiona/ Choices	Does not respond to what is said or done No verbal attention given Physically excludes others (turns back, walks away) No visual attention given	Verbally acknowledges what is said or done Makes direct or indirect statements (can be in agreement or disagreement) Physically acknowledges what is said or done (nods head) Visual attention given	Actively supports decisions or choices made by others Encourages others to make decisions or choices Integrates decisions or choices into group process
Behaviors	Does not respond No verbal attention given Physically excludes others (turns back, walks away) No visual attention given	Verbally acknowledges what is said or done Makes direct or indirect statements (can be in agreement or disagreement) Physically acknowledges what is said or done (nods head) Visual attention given	Allows different behaviors Supports different behaviors Encourages contributions from others Integrates self into group process
Physical	Does not respond appropriately to physical differences (is not helpful or is over-acknowledging)	Makes appropriate verbal comments Makes physical adjustments as necessary	Integrates self into group process Physically supports and encourages others Verbally supports and encourages others

Community Rubric – Individual Assessment

	Level 1	Level 2	Level 3	Level 4
Recognition of Group Members	Positively acknow edge few people in group (e.g., shows little capacity to use names/greetings or know something about group members)	Recognizes some group members in a positive manner	Positively acknowledges most people in group	Positively acknowledges each person in group
Work Together	Little or no effort made to establish positive working relationships with group members	Sometimes makes effort to establish positive working relationships with group members	Establishes positive working relationships with group members most of the time	Establishes positive working relationships with group members all of the time
Safe Environment (Physical)	Little or no effort made, through actions or words, to create or maintain a safe physical environment (lack of attention to safe procedures)	Some effort made, through actions and words, to create and maintain a safe physical environment	Effort is made most of the time, through actions and words, to create and maintain a safe physical environment	Effort is always made, through actions and words, to create and maintain a safe physical environment
Safe Environment (Emotional)	Little or no effort made, through actions or words, to create or maintain a safe emotional environment (use of put—downs)	Some effort made, through actions and words, to create and maintain a safe emotional environment	Effort is made most of the time, through actions and words, to create and maintain a safe emotional environment	Effort is always made, through actions and words, to create and maintain a safe emotional environment
Personal Goals vs. Team Goals	Shows little or no differentiation between individual goals and those of group	Shows occasional differentiation between individual goals and those of group	Mostly shows appropriate differentiation between individual goals and those of group, and can distinguish when it is appropriate to focus on personal or team goals	Always shows appropriate differentiation between individual goals and those of group, and can distinguish when it is appropriate to focus on personal or team goals

Problem Solving — Group Assessment Checklist

	Never (0)	Some of the time (1)	Most of the time (2)	All of the time (3)
Leadership roles are clearly identifiable during the activity.				
Leadership roles are carried out effectively during the activity.				
Followership roles are clearly identifiable during the activity.				
Followership roles are carried out effectively during the activity.				
New ideas are generated by members of the group during the activity.				
New ideas are listened to by members of the group during the activity.				
New ideas are tried by the group during the activity.				
The group evaluates its process during the activity.				
The group makes changes in strategies being used during the activity.				
The group incorporates its prior experiences in the activity.				
The group deals with failure during the activity in a positive manner.				
The group uses physically safe procedures during the activity.				
The group uses emotionally safe procedures during the activity.				
The group makes use of the various strengths of its members during the activity.				
TOTAL SCORE				

Compassion – Peer Assessment

Your Name _____ Date _____

Name of Partner _____

	Not at all true			Very True
1. Gives physical help to others in the group when they need it.	1	2	3	4
2. Gives encouragement to others in the group when they need it.	1	2	3	4
3. Cares about the physical safety of others in the group.	1	2	3	4
4. Cares about the emotional safety of others in the group.	1	2	3	4
5. Accepts the choices made by others in the group.	1	2	3	4
6. Is open to suggestions made by others in the group.	1	2	3	4

Self-Concept – Self-Assessment

Name _____

Date _____

I solve my problems quite easily.	Yes	No
I share my ideas with the others in my group.	Yes	No
I share my feelings with the others in my group.	Yes	No
I get along well with other people.	Yes	No
I take appropriate physical risks.	Yes	No
I take appropriate emotional risks.	Yes	No
I feel good most of the time.	Yes	No
I pay attention during group activities.	Yes	No
I am a safe person.	Yes	No
I am an honest person.	Yes	No
I set goals for myself that I can achieve.	Yes	No
I can let go and move on after conflicts.	Yes	No

Respect for Differences – Journal Questions

1. What has your group done to show respect for the differences that people bring to class? Use examples to support your answer.

2. What actions have you taken that show your respect for differences? Are there any examples of when you did not show respect for differences? Be specific.

3. Have your strengths been valued by the individuals in your group? Use examples to support your answer.

4. How does the Full Value Contract help the group respect differences? Give examples.

Community – Journal Questions

1. When have you felt emotionally and physically safe in this class? When have you felt unsafe? In your examples, explain what contributed to your feeling safe and unsafe.

2. In what ways do you help create a physically and emotionally safe environment in this class? Use examples to support your answer.

3. List the names of the students in this class and something that you know about each one.

4. In this last activity [insert appropriate activity here], when did you see people being cooperative? When did you see them being competitive? Use specific examples to support your answer.

Self-Esteem – Journal Questions

1. What are some words you would use to describe yourself? Why did you pick these words?

2. What are some things you are good at? Are there things that you are good at now that you were not as good at in elementary school? Support your examples with specific information.

3. How do you react when you succeed at something you have put effort into? How do you react when you do not succeed at something you have put effort into? Support your answer with examples.

4. How does peer pressure affect the decisions you make?

STUDENT COMMUNITY SURVEY

This is an assessment tool that will be generated by the students in your class. Consider giving the class a specific question/topic to survey, such as, "How has our community developed since the beginning of this unit?" This assessment offers an opportunity for students to collaborate with a math teacher.

Directions:

- Divide the class into groups of three or four.
- Each team is responsible for creating a list of questions (between 5 and 10) that relate to the topic.
- Once their list of questions has been generated, each team then approaches other students in the class to get answers.
- After the surveys are complete and data gathered, each group compiles their results.
- Groups take turns presenting their findings to the class.

RESPECT FOR DIFFERENCES — PROJECT

In doing this project, students will look at examples of differences that exist in their community and in the world, and they will examine how these differences affect various activities and tasks.

Time Needed

Part of a class period to introduce the project; homework or class time for groups to work on the project, class time for presentations.

Group Size

The project should be done in small groups of not fewer than two but no more than four students each.

The Project:

1. Divide students into small "project groups." In their groups, have them brainstorm times during their physical education classes where differences have existed among participants. Each group should then share with the rest of the class their examples of differences.

2. Groups can then identify other situations where differences do exist—or might exist—among people. These examples can be real or hypothetical; they can be taken from the school setting or from the world in general. Using their chosen examples, student groups are to identify the specific differences that exist and how these differences could affect (or have affected), either positively or negatively, the situation or activity being done.

You might choose to assign students to find an article from a newspaper or magazine in which obvious differences exist among the people involved. Groups would identify these differences and discuss how they have influenced the given situation, as reported in the article. They should next come up with alternative ways in which the differences might have been addressed, treated or incorporated by the people involved, and what effect these alternatives might have had on the outcome.

Another possibility would be to have students choose a picture or advertisement. In this case, groups should create a story about the situation that their image (or ad) seems to depict. Their stories should explain the differences they have identified and how these differences might affect what is happening. They should come up with various ways in which the differences could be addressed, treated or incorporated into the situation and how this could change the outcome.

3. Finally, have each group present their example to the rest of the class. This can be done with a poster, skit, role-playing, "news-type" reporting or another manner that has been preapproved by you.

REFERENCES FOR ASSESSMENT SECTION

Danielson, Charlotte, and Thomas L. McGreal. *Teacher Evaluation: To Enhance Professional Practice.* Alexandria, VA: ASCD, 2000.

Educators in Connecticut's Pomperaug Regional School District 15. *A Teacher's Guide to Performance—Based Learning and Assessment.* Alexandria, VA: ASCD, 1996.

Lewin, Larry, and Betty Jean Shoemaker. *Great Performances: Creating Classroom—Based Assessment Tasks.* Alexandria, VA: ASCD, 1998.

Lund, JaclynLea, Ph.D. *Creating Rubrics for Physical Education.* Alexandria, VA: National Association for Sport and Physical Education, 2000.

Wiggins, Grant, and Jay McTighe. *Understanding by Design.* Alexandria, VA: ASCD, 1998.

Middle School
Appendices

APPENDIX 1: GLOSSARY OF TERMS

Assessment: The systematic gathering of data used to make inferences about student progress in achieving designated learning outcomes based on various sources of evidence

Curriculum: A complete program of learning which includes the following components:

- Identified, desired results
- A design for, and suggested sequence of, activities
- Suggested methods of assessment for evaluation

Desired Results: The overarching understandings and basic information students should know, as well as skills they should be able to use, as the result of a given program; these take into account the developmental needs of students of differing ages and are clearly identified in the curriculum.

Evaluation: The process of judging the quality, value or worth of a program or student performance based upon established criteria, using the data gathered in assessment.

Learning Outcomes: The specific information or skills that are the focus of student learning during a given lesson.

Lesson: A part of a unit, generally presented in one or two days.

Unit: A part of a curriculum with one particular focus

APPENDIX 2:
DESIRED RESULTS OF THE K-12 ADVENTURE PROGRAM

1. Demonstrate an understanding of movement concepts and the use of motor skills.

Grades K–2

- Establish a beginning movement vocabulary as it applies to Adventure activities.
- Acquire basic skills to be applied to activities and games.
- Explore and adapt fundamental movement skills to meet a variety of challenges.
- Use a variety of manipulative, locomotor and nonlocomotor skills as individuals and in teams.
- Use concepts of space awareness and movement control with a variety of basic skills while interacting with others during Adventure activities.
- Use feedback to improve performance.

Grades 3–5

- Adapt a skill to the demands of a dynamic, unpredictable environment.
- Combine movement skills in applied settings.
- Recognize and apply concepts that impact the quality of increasingly complex movement performance.
- Use information from a variety of internal and external sources to improve performance.

Grades 6–8

- Demonstrate increasing competence in more advanced specialized skills.
- Adapt and combine skills to the demands of increasingly complex situations of selected movement forms.
- Recognize general characteristics of movement that can be applied to specific settings.
- Use combinations of manipulative, locomotor and nonlocomotor skills to develop movement sequences and patterns, both individually and with others.
- Identify the critical elements of more advanced movement skills.

Grades 9–12

- Demonstrate competence in an increasing number of more complex versions of movement forms and motor skills as they relate to Adventure activities.
- Use more specialized knowledge to develop movement competence or proficiency.
- Identify and apply critical elements to enable the development of movement competence/proficiency.
- Understand and independently apply discipline-specific information to performance.
- Understand how sport psychology affects the performance of physical activities (e.g., the effect of anxiety on performance).
- Exhibit a level of competency, advancing to a level of proficiency in a particular skill (e.g., belaying, knot tying). Perform basic skills with consistency in the Adventure setting.

2. Demonstrate responsible personal and social behaviors.

Grades K-2

- Understand the purpose of rules in games.
- Apply, with teacher reinforcement, classroom rules and procedures and safe practices.
- Share space and equipment safely and with others.
- Work cooperatively with another to complete an assigned task.

Grades 3-5

- Follow, with few reminders, activity-specific rules, procedures and etiquette.
- Utilize safety principles in activity situations.
- Work cooperatively with a partner or small group.
- Work independently and on-task for short periods of time.
- Identify the various feelings that most people experience, and describe the physical and emotional reactions of the body to intense positive and negative feelings.
- Know behaviors that communicate care, consideration and respect of self and others.
- Understand how one responds to the behavior of others and how one's behavior may evoke responses in others.

Grades 6-8

- Participate in establishing rules, procedures and etiquette that are safe and effective for activity-specific situations.
- Work cooperatively and productively in a group to accomplish a set goal in both cooperative and competitive activities.
- Make conscious decisions about applying rules, procedures and etiquette.
- Use time effectively to complete assigned tasks.
- Understand the physical and environmental dangers associated with particular activities and demonstrate proper procedures for safe participation in Adventure activities.
- Identify and describe the experience of different feelings and how feelings affect daily functioning.
- Understand proper attitudes toward both winning and losing.

Grades 9-12

- Apply safe practices, rules, procedures and etiquette in all Adventure activities.
- Act independently of peer pressure.
- Keep the importance of winning and losing in perspective relative to other established goals of participation.
- Initiate independent and responsible personal behavior in Adventure settings.
- Anticipate potentially dangerous consequences and outcomes of participation in Adventure activities.

3. Demonstrate the ability to use effective interpersonal skills.

Grades K-2

- Understand the elements of socially acceptable conflict resolution in Adventure settings (e.g., cooperation, sharing, consideration).
- Identify different types of communication (e.g., verbal and nonverbal).
- Identify why communication is essential in human relationships.
- Describe some of the ways in which young children can be intentionally helpful and intentionally hurtful to one another.

Grades 3-5

- Apply both verbal and nonverbal communication skills to develop positive relationships.
- Demonstrate self-control and the ability to cope with both success and failure.
- Work constructively with others to accomplish a variety of goals and tasks.
- Develop skills needed for peacefully resolving conflicts in socially acceptable ways.
- Know the difference between positive and negative behaviors used in conflict situations.
- Explain factors that could escalate and reduce conflict.
- Identify the effects of leadership skills on the promotion of teamwork.
- Describe the concept of friendship, and contrast qualities that strengthen or weaken a friendship.
- Know strategies for resisting negative peer pressure.

Grades 6-8

- Apply attentive listening, feedback and assertiveness skills to enhance positive interpersonal communication.
- Describe and demonstrate necessary elements of conflict resolution (e.g., nature of conflict, feelings, active listening, "I" messages and restating), and show effective communication skills in general.
- Work constructively with others to accomplish a goal in a group activity, demonstrating consideration for others involved.
- Understand the role of Adventure activities as a possible arena in which to develop and sharpen leadership skills.
- Analyze the possible causes of conflict among youth in schools and communities.
- Explain how peer pressure influences choices, and apply strategies for managing both negative and positive peer pressure.
- Demonstrate effective communication, negotiation and conflict resolution for resolving potentially violent conflicts.
- Know appropriate ways to build and maintain positive relationships with peers, parents and other adults.
- Know techniques for seeking help and support through appropriate resources.

Grades 9-12

- Define the functions of leadership in Adventure activities.
- Apply conflict-resolution skills appropriately.
- Use leadership and follower roles, when appropriate, in accomplishing group goals in Adventure activities.
- Identify techniques for handling anger and resolving conflicts in family, friendships and workplace settings.
- Explain the purpose of friendship, and describe how friends can support one another in making healthy decisions.
- Identify character traits associated with peaceful living in society, such as respect, tolerance, honesty, self-discipline, kindness and empathy.
- Apply skills to communicate effectively with family, friends and others, and understand the effects of open and honest communication.
- Work constructively with others to accomplish a goal in a group activity, demonstrating consideration for others involved.

4. **Demonstrate the ability to use the decision-making skills of appropriate goal setting, risk taking and problem solving.**

Grades K-2

- Know ways to seek assistance when needed.
- Identify behaviors that are safe or risky.

Grades 3-5

- Demonstrate the steps involved in good decision-making and refusal skills.
- Explain and practice a model for decision making that includes gathering information, predicting outcomes, listing advantages and disadvantages, identifying moral complications and evaluating decisions.
- Know methods used to recognize and avoid threatening situations and ways to get assistance.
- Know behaviors that are safe, risky or harmful to self and others.
- Use decision making, refusal skills and goal setting in an Adventure arena.

Grades 6-8

- Analyze potential consequences when confronted with a behavior choice.
- Describe the contribution of a personal support system to good mental health.
- Understand the difference between safe and risky or harmful behaviors in relationships.
- Implement decision-making skills, refusal skills and goal setting to avoid risky situations.
- Solve problems by analyzing causes and potential solutions.

Grades 9-12

- Anticipate and avoid potentially dangerous situations in Adventure settings.
- Develop and practice effective coping skills for managing stress to prevent self-destructive behaviors.
- Identify ways in which decision making is influenced by sound character, family and personal beliefs.
- Explain positive techniques for handling difficult decisions.
- Demonstrate skills for refusal, negotiation and collaboration to avoid potentially harmful situations in personal, work and community relationships.
- Understand the short- and long-term consequences of both safe and risky or harmful behaviors.

5. **Understand the potential outcomes for participating in Adventure activities, including challenge, enjoyment, self-expression and social interaction.**

Grades K-2

- Engage in physical activities.
- Gain competence to realize increased enjoyment in movement.
- Associate positive feelings with participation in Adventure activities.
- Try new movement activities and skills.
- Identify and share feelings in appropriate ways.
- Express feelings about and during Adventure activities.
- Enjoy interaction with friends through Adventure activities.

Grades 3-5

- Experience enjoyment while participating in Adventure activities.
- Enjoy practicing activities to increase skill competence.
- Interact with friends while participating in group activities.
- Use Adventure activities as a means of self-expression.
- Understand that Adventure activities provide personal challenge.
- Apply methods to accommodate a variety of feelings in a constructive manner in order to promote well-being.

Grades 6-8

- Recognize Adventure activities as a positive opportunity for social and group interaction.
- Demonstrate enjoyment from participation in Adventure activities.
- Use Adventure activities to express feelings.
- Seek personally challenging experiences in physical activity and Adventure opportunities.
- Identify factors that promote a positive self-image (e.g., accepting responsibility; respect for self, authority and others; self-discipline, self-control and the right to be assertive).

- Understand long-term psychological benefits of regular participation in Adventure activities.
- Exhibit openness to try new and different types of activities.

Grades 9-12

- Enjoy participating in a variety of Adventure activities.
- Pursue new activities, both alone and with others.
- Enjoy working with others in an Adventure activity to achieve a common goal.
- Recognize that Adventure activities can provide a positive social environment for activities with others.
- Display heightened self-confidence through participation in Adventure activities.
- Identify and display factors that promote a positive self-image (e.g., accepting responsibility; respect for self, authority and others; self-discipline, self-control and the right to be assertive).
- Understand that Adventure activities can provide opportunities to demonstrate leadership and problem-solving skills.
- Use Adventure activities to express feelings.
- Seek personally challenging experiences in physical activity and Adventure opportunities.
- Understand long-term psychological benefits of regular participation in Adventure activities.
- Exhibit openness to try new and different types of activities.

6. Demonstrate an understanding of and respect for differences.

Grades K-2

- Recognize the joy of shared play.
- Play and cooperate with others regardless of personal differences.
- Treat others with respect during play.
- Understand individual similarities and differences (in terms of appearance and behavior).

Grades 3-5

- Explore cultural/ethnic self-awareness through participation in Adventure activities.
- Recognize the attributes that individuals with differences can bring to group activities.
- Accept teammates regardless of ability, and treat opponents with respect and courtesy.
- Define intolerance and explain how it can be harmful.
- Understand the role of Adventure in learning more about others of both like and different backgrounds.
- Understand the physical challenges faced by people with disabilities.

Grades 6-8

- Acknowledge differences in the behaviors of people of different genders, cultures, ethnicities and disabilities, and seek to learn more about both similarities and differences.
- Cooperate with disabled peers and those of different genders, races and ethnicities.
- Understand and respect the contributions of others with both like and different skill levels to the group or team goal.
- Work cooperatively with both more and less skilled peers.
- Identify behaviors that are inclusive and supportive, as well as those that are exclusionary and not supportive, in Adventure settings.
- Willingly join others of diverse cultures, ethnicities and races during Adventure activities.
- Demonstrate strategies for inclusion of all students in Adventure settings.

Grades 9-12

- Invite others with differences to join in personally enjoyable Adventure activities.
- Recognize the influence of participation in Adventure activities on fostering appreciation of cultural, ethnic, gender and physical diversity.
- Develop strategies for including persons from diverse backgrounds and characteristics in the Adventure activities they select.
- Describe the influence of the larger social group on individual conduct.

APPENDIX 3: WARMUPS

Warmups serve three primary purposes in Adventure programming:

- Emotionally preparing students for an activity
- Physiologically preparing students' bodies for an activity
- Giving teachers important information to use as they apply GRABBSS

Emotional Considerations

Some Adventure activities can be very stressful for individuals. Warmups can set a tone for a class by helping to create an atmosphere of safety. Be sure to do warmups that are supportive in nature before doing an activity that will require a lot of support for individuals in the class. If you are planning a very playful day, create very playful warmups. However, sometimes mixing up more playful warmups with a more serious activity creates a nice balance for the day. Most of all, we encourage you to be thoughtful in what you do during every stage of your Adventure programming.

Physical touching/physical contact are important to mention in this appendix. It is easy to take some of the touching required in these activities for granted (e.g., "OK, everyone hold hands with your partner," or "The class will catch you and gently put you on the ground"). These are all things that are said fairly automatically in the framing of activities. However, that type of physical contact may not be OK for everyone in the class. A good series of warmups slowly introduces touch in nonthreatening ways. First, do activities that require tagging, which might then lead into linking elbows, which could then lead to grabbing hands, etc., before heading off to do a Trust Fall, for example. Warmups can emotionally prepare students for the upcoming task.

Physiological Considerations

As physical educators, you know a great deal about how to physically prepare students for a particular activity. This curriculum is not meant to cover the content required to properly understand the physiology of warmups. However, included here are some key considerations for educators to focus on while programming with Adventure.

- **Raise students' pulses slightly before stretching.** Stretching a cold muscle is like trying to squeeze a dry sponge. Students need to get blood into their muscles to literally warm them up before trying to stretch them out.

- **Stretch, focusing on specific body parts and areas that will be stressed or used in the activity.** So often we see Adventure programmers who are not physical educators move from activity to activity without properly adding stretches that might prevent injury. Teach proper stretching techniques to your students—these stretching activities can be fun—and take the time to add more stretches throughout the class if needed. We suggest an emphasis on shoulder stretches if students will be climbing and doing many of the low elements. It is also important to emphasize lower body stretching when doing many other games and initiatives.

- **Prepare students for future physiological needs in warmups.** If you know that swing ropes will be used later in the program, for example, add arm-strengthening opportunities to your warmups.

Help with Applying GRABBSS

During the warmup phase of a lesson, make a note of key pieces of information that can help you with activity selection or reselection, framing ideas, even rule variations. Classes have moods; a teacher can observe the mood of a class as students act especially playful in a warmup, for instance, or as they ignore the Full Value Contract in a tag game, or as they move carefully in a running activity.

What we mean by this is simple. Try to use warmups that are fun and engaging. A list is provided here for your reference. The key activity of every lesson will be much more successful if students are properly warmed up and if they are in the spirit of Adventure before beginning. And, remember this simple concept: **Use warm-ups that are appropriate to Adventure programming.**

There are literally hundreds of warm-ups that can be used. Following is a sample list of reliable warm-ups; these are referenced in some Project Adventure publications (listed in the right column of the chart that follows).

Activity Name	Publication Reference
1. Back to Earth	Cowstails II
2. Bottoms-Up Stretch	Cowstails II
3. Como Esta Usted?	Back Pocket Adventure
4. Copy Cat	Quicksilver
5. Dog Shake	Silver Bullets
6. Everybody's Up	Adventures in Peacemaking
7. Impulse	Cowstails II
8. Inchworm	Cowstails II
9. King Frog	Adventures in Peacemaking
10. Mrs. O'Grady	Silver Bullets
11. Pass the Shoe	Adventures in Peacemaking
12. Red Baron Stretch	Cowstails II
13. Robart Tag	Back Pocket Adventure
14. Row Boat Stretch	Cowstails II
15. Sacky Hack	Silver Bullets
16. Stork Stretch	Silver Bullets
17. Triangle Tag	Silver Bullets
18. Twelve Hours of Cooperation	Adventures in Peacemaking
19. Wamsamsam	Back Pocket Adventure
20. Weird Walkin'	Back Pocket Adventure
21. Wiz Bang	Quicksilver

APPENDIX 4: DEBRIEFING

The doing of a particular activity can be powerful. Likewise, reflecting on and debriefing about the activity can be enlightening. An experiential educator needs to use a balance of both doing and reflecting to make teaching and learning most effective. Recall the Experiential Learning Cycle that was described in the Introduction. This theoretical model highlights the role of the debrief as a chance for a number of key things to occur. These include replaying important moments in the activity so that everyone is reminded of what actually happened, and forming some generalizations about behaviors and team or individual performance. The final step in this process is helping students to understand how to transfer these generalizations to other activities—and, most importantly, to other real-life situations.

Facilitation of the Experiential Learning Cycle process is often referred to as the *Adventure Wave.*

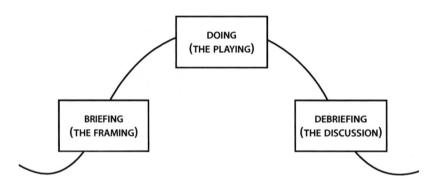

The Adventure Wave is a simple way of describing the steps that are already designed and incorporated into each lesson. The start of the Wave is the Brief or Framing of the activity. This sets the stage for what is to be done, in essence creating the atmosphere. The Doing or Playing is the actual performance/execution of the activity. The end of the Wave is the Debrief or Discussion period, that critical step where students are given an opportunity to glean important learning from what they have done. Not every individual game needs to go through this Wave, but every lesson or series of games should. As educators become more comfortable with Adventure activities, it becomes easier for them to know when to take the time to step back and reflect and when it is better to move on. Overprocessing can be as deadly as underprocessing.

Discussion is the most prevalent debriefing technique used in Adventure education today. It is also the most common technique that is overused. A good discussion session can be terrific. Yet, if done after every activity, with no other medium through which students can express themselves, those who are uncomfortable about speaking to the group, auditory learners and nonverbal learners can be lost. Discussion, day in and day out, can also get boring. So, a balanced approach is often the most effective way in which to keep students' interest in the reflection aspect of the Adventure Wave. As mentioned in the Introduction, the Debrief should review the basic themes of "What happened?", "So what about what has occurred?", and the critical transfer, "Now what do we do with this information?"

After each activity in this book a list of discussion questions is included. These can serve as topic suggestions that can either be discussed or explored in a variety of different ways. Following are some of the different ways in which to approach a Debrief.

Debriefing Techniques

TRIADS AND DYADS: The difference between talking in front of a large class versus talking to a partner is dramatic for many students. Splitting the class into twos or threes is a wonderful way to gain more participation in the discussion. Often, it is effective to have small groups share key points of their discussions with the larger class.

VIDEO: Ask the class to close their eyes while you do a brief guided imagery of the initiative that you are debriefing. As you guide them through the factual review of what happened, ask students to "stop the video," mentally and silently, on a particular frame that is poignant for them individually. The frame should be relevant to the theme you are focusing on. When your imagery is done, ask students to share with the class the frames that they have selected.

SNAPSHOT: As in the video technique above, ask students to reflect silently on the past initiative. Individually, they are to take a mental snapshot of a key moment, frame it in a particular frame, and then verbally present this snapshot to the class.

PLAY DOUGH: Nonverbal students often love this. Ask each person or small group to create a play dough representation to answer a question posed or to illustrate their reaction or thoughts on an activity or event.

PIPE CLEANERS: Easier to store and less messy than play dough, pipe cleaners can serve the same function as play dough.

FEELINGS MARKETPLACE CARDS: These are a "must have" in your Adventure bag of tricks. This series of cards, each with a feeling creatively written on it, are very versatile. In general, they offer students a choice of words to select to help them share or explain their emotions about whatever you are debriefing. The cards can be selected to describe oneself, given to someone else as a feedback tool, to describe the class or the group, etc. Be creative with these cards.

STATUE OR POSTURE: Kinesthetic learners will be engaged when asked to stand in postures or as statues to describe their reflections on an activity. Small-group and full-class statues are effective as well.

JOURNALS: Journal writing can be both an assessment tool and a reflection tool. Asking students to spend time reflecting in their journals, and then verbally sharing key points with partners or the class, can help those who are comfortable with writing to share their thoughts with the group. If journaling is used, be sure to tell people before they write that they will be asked to share their thoughts. If you are collecting the journals, do not correct for grammar and spelling. Let the journals be a place where students feel free to express themselves.

BUMPER STICKERS OR HEADLINERS: Have students create individual bumper stickers or newspaper headlines that capture the performance of the class (or other situations you may assign). Providing colorful markers makes this an even more creative outlet for the artists in the class.

HIGH-LOW, QUICK WHIPS, ONE WORD: These are all large- or small-group debriefing techniques that can vary the typical discussion format. They are often used after completing high challenge course activities. For High-Low, ask each person to describe his or her personal high for an activity, and then the personal low. Quick Whips and One Word debriefs involve simply asking students to quickly say the one word or sentence that describes what they felt about a particular event or activity.

DEBRIEFING TIPS FOR TEACHERS

1. Don't be afraid of debriefing. Students will talk, share and reflect if given the right tools.

2. Be flexible. If one question does not elicit any response, ask a different one or use a different technique.

3. Don't overprocess. Sometimes it is more powerful to just move on to the next activity, allowing the group to transfer their learning naturally.

4. Use a circle. Creating a physical setting that allows for good discussion and sharing is important. Standing or sitting in rows, or with some students not able to see others, can create a negative environment.

5. Try new things. Don't get caught just asking questions. Give some of the above suggestions a try!

6. Don't ask, "How did that make you feel?" over and over again. Feeling questions are hard to answer.

7. Be playful even in the Debrief. The discussion does not have to be heavy.

8. Be careful of any cans of worms you may open. If a Debrief begins to get heavy, make sure that you have the skills—and the time—to manage or terminate the topic appropriately.

9. Stay focused on the lesson outcomes when preparing questions. Keep the goals of the activity in mind as you design the Debrief.

10. **Listen.** Students will have a lot to say and will say it in different ways. Listen.

ACTIVITY LIST (alphabetical)

ABOUT THE AUTHORS

Jane Panicucci, M.Ed., Harvard University, is currently Director of Training and Consulting for Project Adventure. Jane's Adventure background includes 11 years as a course director at Outward Bound. In the mid 80s, as a public school physical educator, Jane designed an Adventure curriculum that is still going strong. Her current consulting specialties include working with teachers and administrators to generate positive change in their schools and to create high-performing teams for both non-profit and for-profit organizations.

Lisa Faulkingham Hunt is a Project Adventure trainer specializing in youth programs as well as professional development. She brings her passion for activities and her belief in their outcomes to her work with both youth and adult groups. Lisa has a degree in Anthropology from Lewis and Clark College in Portland, OR.

Amy Kohut has been an Adventure Educator for 22 years. She has a Health and Physical Education degree from West Chester University in West Chester, PA. Over the years she has worked for Princeton University, the Appalachian Mountain Club, Outward Bound, and is currently the Manager of School and Community Programs for Project Adventure.

Alison Rheingold, M.Ed., Lesley College (with a focus on special needs students), has used experiential teaching methods in a variety of settings including traditional classrooms, Outward Bound, residential camps, and environmental education day camps. She is currently a full-time trainer and consultant for Project Adventure.

Nancy Stratton (Constable), M.Ed., Harvard University, has had numerous roles within traditional as well as alternative schools for over 30 years. She currently works on special projects with Project Adventure as well as professional development with teachers and curriculum development with school systems.

 Project Adventure, Inc.

ABOUT PROJECT ADVENTURE

Project Adventure is a nonprofit, international teaching organization that is committed to providing leadership in the use of experiential programming to promote individual growth, effective organizations and healthy communities.

Project Adventure offers the following services. For more information, check our web site at **www.pa.org.**

Open Enrollment and Custom Training

Challenge Course Design

Program Safety Services

Publications

Equipment

Custom Youth Programs

Project Adventure Corporate Office

701 Cabot St.
Beverly, MA 01915
(978) 524-4500

Workshop Registrations: 1-800-468-8898
Catalog/Publications: 1-800-796-9917